"Jesus has never accepted mediocrity. He calls passionate followers. In *A Heart on Fire*, my dear friend Glen Berteau provides a necessary spark for those growing indifferent toward their faith and who need revival."

—John Bevere, bestselling author and minister, cofounder of Messenger International

"I know Pastor Glen Berteau. I know him well, having tag-teamed with him in ministry in Australia, New Zealand and the US. I visited him in the hospital shortly after his super-natural resurrection. He's the real deal. His words are not to occupy time and space, but rather to transform lives. *A Heart on Fire* will do that for you and those you love."

—Sam Chand, president of Samuel R. Chand Consulting

"Evil presses two lies on the church today. The first lie is that revival is unattainable. The second lie is that one single believer cannot change the world. Both lies are destroyed in the deeply inspirational and motivating book *A Heart on Fire* by Glen Berteau."

—Mario Murillo, journalist, author, teacher

A
HEART
ON
FIRE

A HEART ON FIRE

YOU ARE CHOSEN TO CHANGE THE WORLD

GLEN BERTEAU

Chosen

a division of Baker Publishing Group
Minneapolis, Minnesota

Published by Chosen Books
Minneapolis, Minnesota
www.chosenbooks.com

Chosen Books is a division of
Baker Publishing Group, Grand Rapids, Michigan

Printed in the United States of America

ISBN 978-0-8007-9965-6 (trade paper)
ISBN 978-1-4934-3715-3 (ebook)
ISBN 978-0-8007-6312-1 (casebound)
Library of Congress Control Number: 2022038645

Cover design by Nellie Nous

Author represented by The Bindery, LLC

Baker Publishing Group publications use paper produced from sustainable forestry practices and post-consumer waste whenever possible.

23   24   25   26   27   28   29   7   6   5   4   3   2   1

Contents

Foreword

Terror, economic fluctuations, homelessness, addictions, suicide, the sexualization of children, human trafficking. What is the answer to the world's problems and the malaise, angst, and consternation we live with in today's generation?

The answer is not political. The only solution is our Lord Jesus. We need revival. Imagine if the Holy Spirit of God came in a wave of glory flowing from California to Florida and hit all points in between. I believe this kind of outpouring of the Holy Spirit is on the way.

The question for you and me is, will we participate? Or will we merely be spectators of that revival?

Glen Berteau's book, *A Heart on Fire*, walks readers through what is required to become part of, or even become the start of, this revival. Glen writes, "Revival does not happen outside until it happens inside. Something has got to happen inside you so that it can ultimately happen in our cities and nation."

I couldn't agree more. In Scripture, we read that Elijah found Elisha plowing a field. Elijah went to Elisha and threw his mantle across Elisha's shoulders. In this story, the plow represents the perseverance of work and sowing seed, and the mantle represents promotion. The subtext is that if you can push the plow, you can carry the mantle.

Elijah and Elisha lived in an era much like ours today. It was a generation marked by two wicked rulers. Ahab was a horrible king, and his wife Jezebel hated and persecuted the prophets of God. Spiritually speaking, Ahab represents forces with access and authority who sacrifice truth on the altar of expediency. Jezebel represents a manipulative, sexually coercive, perverse, corrupt cultural spirit intended to kill the prophetic voices, silence truth and marginalize the oracles of righteousness and justice.

I believe we live in a generation threatened by the same spirit today. Yet, I believe the "roaring twenties" of this millennium will be marked by the same spirit that promoted Elijah and Elisha. This generation of Elijahs and Elishas will be empowered by the Holy Spirit. They will exalt the name of Jesus, and with hands to the plow, they will usher in a fresh move of God's Spirit.

What is the most powerful spirit alive today? It's not the spirit of Jezebel. It's not the spirit of Ahab. The most powerful spirit alive today is still the Holy Spirit of our God. When the Holy Spirit of God revives us personally on the inside, every other spirit is driven out.

Glen writes in this book, "A personal revival is not going to change who you are; it is going to remove who you are not."

The Holy Spirit removes our issues, our prejudices, our unforgiveness, our cowardice, our hurts and wounds. As we push the plow every day, pressing into Jesus, pursuing passionately the presence of God, God's mantle will fall on us.

Today's plow pushers are tomorrow's mantle carriers. For this reason, we cannot mistake the temporary for the permanent. We cannot think the process is the promise. We cannot confuse what we're going through with where we're going to.

Glen starts with the words "You have been chosen to change the world." It's true. You have. So I encourage you to read on, then go do it.

Reverend Samuel Rodriguez

Introduction

I Am Revival

O*Lord, let revival begin in me!* This desire was ignited in me and has been smoldering and burning since the day I was saved—49 years ago.

On November 25, 2019, I had a sudden cardiac arrest and died sitting in the front seat of my car in my church parking lot. Paramedics attempted to resuscitate me for 45 minutes before they found a slight pulse. I died and was revived eight times. It is a supernatural miracle that I am alive today.

Recovery has been the most difficult task that I have had to overcome. I must remind myself daily that God has more for me to accomplish. He wants me to speak into lives, to stir men and women to believe in Him, to develop a deep relationship with Him and to live a revival lifestyle.

The days of Oral Roberts and the old healing evangelists has ended, and we have a younger generation that is void of seeing signs, wonders and miracles. I believe the next revival will not only be souls but biblical miracles. As you read this book, I believe that you will be set on fire for this next revival. I pray it will remind you that you have been chosen to change the world—your world—right where you are.

Too often we think a solution to our problems lies somewhere beyond us. We often believe new government officials, for example, will be the answer to our problems. Our thoughts are formed from watching the news and surfing the internet rather than from reading our Bibles. All that negativity shapes our opinions and the way we think. The state of the world feels chaotic, and we lose the pulse on God's plans and how He can use even the most unqualified individuals to shape history. It is nothing new. Even in Bible times people struggled with seeing beyond the current state of things.

> Oh, what a sinful nation they are—loaded down with a burden of guilt. They are evil people, corrupt children who have rejected the LORD. They have despised the Holy One of Israel and turned their backs on him. Why do you continue to invite punishment? Must you rebel forever? Your head is injured, and your heart is sick. You are battered from head to foot—covered with bruises, welts, and infected wounds—without any soothing ointments or bandages. Your country lies in ruins, and your towns are burned. Foreigners plunder your fields before your eyes and destroy everything they see.
>
> Isaiah 1:4–7

The good news is that we know the only One who can breathe upon this earth and bring revival, unity and hope. Our answers lie in the Word of God if we will just open it and read it. God's story is one of hope. It is one in which everything formed against you is used for your good. It is one in which you can overcome evil with good.

Can you imagine what you could do with a heart full of fire for Jesus? You may not feel as if you have been chosen, but God has predestined you to be a carrier of revival to the world. In order to fulfill your calling, you must accept that God has chosen you for such a time as this. So, how do you start? Where do you begin?

- Start by acknowledging, out loud, that you have been chosen to change the world, your city and your neighborhood.
- Start by being fed up with what is going on in the world. You are the difference-maker.
- Start by healing your heart through the giving and receiving of forgiveness.

A personal revival is not going to change who you are; it is going to remove who you are not. Your desire to succeed must be greater than your fear of failure. When you give God a heart of fire, you will realize your destiny and purpose. You will understand why you are alive right now.

1 | Chosen to Change the World

You have been chosen to change the world.

God ordained you to be a positive influence, an ambassador of the Kingdom of heaven, a carrier of revival to the world. What impact are you making today? Accepting God's call to change the world is a choice only you can make.

In Luke 15, we read a story about a tax collector. Nobody likes to pay their taxes, but tax collectors in Jesus' day were a lot different from our tax collectors. They were nasty people who worked for the Roman Empire. They could tax you two, three or four times more than what you should be taxed. If you did not pay, they could call Roman soldiers to arrest you. That is why Zacchaeus, the tax collector, was considered a snake. Even his "generosity" was made possible by the extortion of others.

Being considered the friend of a tax collector would have cast a negative reflection on you. People thought if you hung around with crooks and criminals, you must be okay with their behavior. You were implicit in taking food out of children's mouths, leaving widows destitute and burdening families with debts they did not deserve and could not pay.

Tax collectors were lumped in with other notorious sinners of the day: social outcasts, prostitutes, drug addicts and the like. The Bible says it was this crew of unlikable individuals who often came to Jesus and listened to Him teach.

Some Christians act as if they are so spiritual that they can only relate to those who float at angel altitude. Let me tell you, it does not work like that. Jesus-followers have the ability to relate to people of the world. That is what we are called to do! We are called to be the light of the world. We are chosen to change the world.

Some Christians act as if the world has a sin-disease they will catch if they get too close. This is not scriptural. Jesus was perfect and sinless, and yet He welcomed the tax collectors and sinners to come and sit with Him. He wanted them to hear Him preach. He knew He was the antidote to their sin-disease, and He was willing to let people into His circle. Because He was willing, lives were healed and changed.

The other day, I was in a drugstore that I frequent often. I went to the desk to check out. The guy behind the counter had this pull-over hairdo and huge gauges that looked like hubcaps in his ears. He was young, maybe twenty, and just weird looking. I did not have a problem with what I just mentioned, but he had a Satanic symbol tattooed on his arm. I thought, *This kid is probably a Satanist or something. Nothing like me, a Christian Jew.*

I looked at his name tag and deliberately started calling him by name. I did not say anything about the star tattoo on his arm, but just kept speaking respectfully and nicely to him. While nothing changed immediately, I will keep going back to the drugstore to look for him. I will continue talking to him and will develop a relationship with him. I believe that sooner or later I am going to be the person who is going to change his world through Jesus Christ.

We cannot run from people of the world. We cannot avoid those who look like sinners and tax collectors. We must welcome them into our presence and get into their presence. We have got to be like Jesus.

The Bible tells us the tax collectors and sinners often came to hear Jesus teach. This offended the Pharisees and the teachers of religious law. They complained that they were being associated with such sinful people because they, too, came to hear Jesus teach. Can you imagine how that would sound from Pharisees today?

"How could Pastor Glen hang out with people who are not saved and then hang out with us? We're Christians!"

"I can't believe that he is hanging out with somebody in the world. Do you see what that kid is wearing?"

"There he is hanging out with a tax collector again."

"He and his wife are eating with a prostitute—a known prostitute!"

"That guy just got out of jail! Pastor Glen is eating chimichangas at La Parrilla with a murderer."

If you saw me around town with a known criminal or bad person, would you think less of me? The religious people thought badly of Jesus because they thought that He should not be hanging around with this sinful crowd.

No, no, no! You have been chosen to change the world. You know who is in the world? Sinners! Sinners are in the world. Bad people.

Parables with a Point

Jesus told the Pharisees and religious leaders a story. He said, "A man had a hundred sheep. One of them got lost. Do you know what the man did? He left the 99 others in the wilderness and went to search for the one that was lost. And then do you know what he did? He carried it back home on his shoulders" (see Luke 15:3–5). Could it be that if 99 believers were in a church service, Jesus would leave the church to find the one who had strayed?

YOU HAVE BEEN CHOSEN TO CHANGE THE WORLD.

I can almost hear Jesus as He looks over the Sunday morning congregation. "Tell them to keep singing, Glen. We've got to go find some sheep. They're not here today."

Imagine if I turned to my staff and said, "I have to go find some lost sheep. I heard they hang out at Starbucks now. I am heading downtown to find them." What if I did not preach because I went to Starbucks to find and bring the lost sheep home? Some members of my church would not like that. They would ask, "Where's Pastor Glen? He's supposed to be here. I don't know what he thinks he's doing. He is talking to one person when we've got thousands here that he needs to talk to. He needs to feed us the Word!" No. You eat too much. You need to start putting your faith into action.

Jesus went on to say that when the man arrived home with his lamb, he called together his friends and neighbors and threw a party (see Luke 15:6). Would we rejoice with the man? What would our response be if someone came to us and said, "Hey, come meet my brother. He has been lost for about ten years, and he has finally come back to the Lord! He's been on drugs, but now he's free!"

Or what if a friend said, "I just reunited with my sister after twenty years. I want her to meet you!" We would be thrilled about that, right? So why would we not be equally thrilled—or even more thrilled—about the lost being found? Jesus said there is more joy in heaven over one sinner who repents and returns to God than over 99 who stay faithful (see Luke 15:7).

He went on to tell the religious leaders another parable. He said, "Suppose a woman has ten silver coins and loses one" (Luke 15:8). The woman lost something? Not the man? Yes. Oh, we are going to start a fight right now! (Don't worry. This is going to turn around.) The value of a coin was about a day's wage. The woman in this story had lost a whole day of pay when she lost that coin. Jesus said, "Won't she light a lamp and sweep the entire house and search carefully until she finds it?" (verse 8).

Imagine that you lost your keys. What are you going to do? You cannot drive your car. You might freak out a little searching for them, but you will search everywhere until you find them, right?

Jesus said that when the woman finds the coin, "She will call in her friends and neighbors and say, 'Rejoice with me because I have found my lost coin'" (verse 9). Would you not do that? He said, "In the same way, there is joy in the presence of God's angels when even one sinner repents" (verse 10).

Lost in Dallas

Let me tell you a man story. I do not lose things often. If I do, I get mad at myself. You know, *Come on, Glen! Where did you put it? This is stupid! What is wrong with you?*

Deborah and I were in Dallas, Texas, where I would be speaking at a church. The pastor and I have been friends for many years. The next day, we were to fly out so that we could get back to our church in time for the evening service. We decided to stop at a fashion jewelry store so that my wife could look around. It was not an exciting stop for me as I typically end up holding my wife's purse. Deborah found several inexpensive pieces of nice jewelry (it looked like a bunch of Mardi Gras beads to me), and like a good husband, I paid for it.

Well, the next morning as I got ready to go to the airport, I realized that I could not find my wallet! Because my license was in the wallet, I really needed to find it. Without it, I was not going to be able get on the plane. I panicked a little.

I looked over there. "Do you see my wallet?"

I looked over here. "Where did you put my wallet?"

I went through bags. "You must have lost it because I don't lose my wallet."

I tossed around the blankets and pillows. "Someone touched it. Yeah, you did, Deborah! You touched it! So where did you put it?!"

I looked all over, but I could not find it. Then I remembered the little jewelry shop. I figured that I must have left it at the counter when I paid.

The jewelry shop did not open till ten o'clock, but we got there thirty minutes early. I could see clearly that the staff was fixing up the store, stocking jewelry and such, but the door was locked. I started banging on the door.

"Hey! I left my wallet in your store! I have to catch a plane!" Nobody would look at me because they had not clocked in yet. They did not care about me or my departure time. Then the lady who had checked me out the night before walked by.

I yelled, "It's you! You, lady! You checked me out yesterday! My wallet is in there! Open the door! We've got a plane to catch!"

She stopped and asked, "What do you want?"

"You checked me out yesterday. Remember? I had to hire a U-Haul to carry out our jewelry. Yeah, that was us. Look, let me in. Check and see if you have my wallet."

She looked in the lockbox, but it was not there. I asked if she had another box. Nope. My wallet was not in the building. It was after ten o'clock at this point, so we headed back to the hotel to look around the room one more time. I was thinking, *Maybe they found it when they cleaned the room. Maybe it is waiting for me at the front desk.* We got to the hotel and learned that they had cleaned our room—but my wallet had not been found.

I called my assistant, Shannen, and said, "We can't get on the plane. I can't find my wallet!" I called my friend and said, "Pray for us. I can't find my wallet!" I called a bunch of people and asked them to pray. Then I opened the trunk and grabbed my briefcase.

There is this one little zipper pocket in my briefcase that I never use. I never put anything in there. Have you done this before? You never put anything in it—except this *one* time? You figure, *If I cannot find it, then whoever breaks into my room will not find it either.* I unzipped this pocket, and there was my wallet, safe and sound.

I took off running to the hotel and told everyone, "I found it! Don't worry!"

I called my assistant and said, "I found it! Don't worry!"

I called my friend and said, "I found it! Don't worry!"

I called everybody.

There is a certain excitement you experience when you find something that you believed was lost. We should have this kind of excitement when somebody walks to the altar to find Jesus. You and I need to shout about it. "They found Him! They found Him! Praise God!"

Charlotte Was Chosen to Change the World

I am glad you are reading this today. I want to tell you about a few people who were lost. All of them decided how they would respond to God's call upon their lives. Some said yes; some said no. Let's see how things turned out for them.

I spoke at a Christian high school years ago. It was not really a Christian school, but it was Christian in name, if you know what I mean. It was a place for everyone, from the Christian student to the student who had been kicked out of public school for misconduct. After I finished speaking, this beautiful student named Charlotte came up to me. She was a talented young lady in many areas, including academics.

From the way she carried herself, you would think she would be the sweetest, nicest person in the world. She came to me and asked if she could meet to talk about something she had been dealing with in her life. Now, normally I would tell someone to go straight to the Lord about whatever he or she is dealing with, but I felt God speak to me about meeting with her. I had her call my office to schedule an appointment. Charlotte came to my office, and what she told me surprised me.

She said, "Four out of five nights a week I wake up with these horrible dreams where I'm dying. I get killed at least four times a week in my dreams. They are violent and horrible dreams."

I asked, "What kind of music do you listen to?" She was not a Christian, so she told me that she listened to death metal. Let me just connect that for you right here: death metal equals death dreams.

I said, "You're listening to horrible people singing about death and demons and hell. They're putting pictures in your mind, and your dreams are coming from the music."

She remarked, "Oh, that's crazy! No way that happens!"

I said, "Yeah, it does. But Charlotte, when I saw you and found out what you do and who you are in this school, I felt prompted to tell you that you're chosen to change the world. You're popular. You're at the top of your class. You've got all these little girls who follow you around. You're an influencer. You've been chosen to change the world. I need to help you understand why you are here. I want to help you understand your purpose."

She said, "No way. I don't believe that, and I don't believe the music has anything to do with my dreams."

I said, "It does. I can pray for you right now, and when Jesus replaces that, you will totally be free. You won't have any more nightmares."

She showed me a sketchbook that held drawings that she had done. The images were quite good, but they were satanic imagery. She said that some were taken from the album art of music that she listened to.

I said, "Wow. Here's the devil. And here's Satan with the staff. No wonder you have these nightmares!" I flipped the page, and one specific demonic image jumped out to me. Charlotte told me that it was a representation of who she was on the inside. It is amazing how we can play the game and look put together on the outside, but when we step into the silence, we realize the ugliness of who we really are. We are not who we pretend to be.

I told Charlotte, "You don't have life in you at all. You have death. You have a spirit of suicide on you." She agreed. "But Charlotte, you've been chosen. You understand what God has done for you? You've been chosen to change the world. Let me pray with you. Let me tell you how this can turn around."

Charlotte said no. She did not believe she was chosen. She left my office, and I did not see her for quite a while. Then one day, she showed up to one of our church meetings.

After the service, she told me, "Hey, you're pretty good at preaching. I really believe you tell the truth. I just don't want to accept it. You do tell the truth, and I like hearing the truth, but I don't want it." When she said that, the Lord told me three specific things that were going to happen in her life. I shared them with her, but I did not tell another human being. She left resistant to what I had said, defiantly dismissing the series of events the Lord showed me she would experience. Over the next several months, each of the things the Lord showed me happened to her. She reached out to me and reported what happened, but still turned her back on the Lord.

I did everything I could to reach that little girl who was chosen to change the world. And she still said no.

Steven Was Chosen to Change the World

Steven was a guy involved in the occult in school. I was getting ready to start a Christian club at his school when he sought me out. He looked as though he was the head of a gang. He had influence. Gang leaders have influence. They can gather people to do all sorts of harmful things. They can tell people, "You go shoot this one, you stab that one." People obey and do it. That influence is something God put in them to use for His glory, but it gets used by the devil.

Steven said to me, "If you go around starting Christian clubs, I'll start satanic clubs in the same school."

I said, "Have at it! We'll see which club wins. But you know that you've been chosen to change the world."

He said, "No. I don't want it." Steven never did start any satanic clubs. In fact, he ended up coming to our church. He later confessed to me that he only came to the service to shoot me, but he saw an angel behind me during the altar call. It radically changed his life.

Change the World

The rich young ruler met Jesus (see Matthew 19:16–23). Here was a person who had everything, and he was chosen to change the world. He had the funds to underwrite everything Jesus did and every church that would start later. He had an audience with the Son of God. Jesus told the rich young ruler what it was going to cost him to follow and that he could change the world if he did. Matthew tells us, "But when the young man heard this, he went away sad, for he had many possessions" (verse 22). He was a man who had the ability to gain wealth, and he had the ability to lead. He led thousands of people, but he could not lead himself.

Judas was chosen, picked by Jesus, to be one of twelve individuals to change the world. He had the opportunity, but you know what? He just could not get himself right. He listened to too much negativity, and he ended up turning Jesus in to the authorities (see Luke 22:3–6). After that, he killed himself.

I think Barabbas would have had a tremendous testimony, don't you? He was released when Jesus was taken captive. He was a murderer. He deserved his jail time. He deserved the cross, but when asked whether they should release Barabbas or Jesus, the people shouted, "Give us Barabbas!" He walked free (see Matthew 27:15–26). You would think that in that moment, this man would realize that he was chosen to change the world. He was given a second chance and a platform. He could have gone from a murderer to a minister. But there is not one Scripture passage that tells us he changed.

Lauren Was Chosen to Change the World

I remember a girl named Lauren in one of the high schools I served. She got saved later in her high school years. She was one of those girls who had slept around because she wanted to feel loved and accepted. One day she realized that her behavior was hurting her, and she had an encounter with the Lord. Her life changed dramatically.

Around that same time, I challenged a group of young people that before they left high school, they needed to make a difference. They needed to let people know who they were. They needed to let others know they were believers who would stand with Christ and not bow out. Lauren was a part of this group, and she listened to my challenge. She determined that she was going to take a great stand when she had the chance.

She found the opportunity during an assignment in which the students were to speak about an item that meant a lot to them. She knew that she wanted to talk about her Bible. She stood in front of the class and told them that her item was the most powerful item in the world. "It has the ability to take a life and change it so that the bad things a person does, he or she will not want to continue doing. It can take health issues, like cancer and heart disease, and heal them in an instant. My item has the ability to release alcoholics or drug addicts."

When she revealed that her item was a Bible, the students vocalized disappointment. "It's a Bible you're talking about?

I thought you had some kind of drug—some new thing that could do all that you said."

She bravely continued, "Hey, you know me. A couple of years ago, I was with most of you doing the things that you did. Then I stopped, but you didn't know why I changed. It was the Man in this Book who changed me. Everything I told you is exactly the truth."

The anointing flooded the classroom, and Lauren told the students that the Author of her Book, Jesus, wanted to change their lives just as He had changed hers. She then asked her teacher if she could ask the class if they wanted to know the Author of her Book, Jesus. With the teacher's approval, Lauren then asked every student to bow their heads and pray. Almost twenty students prayed the sinner's prayer!

We Were Chosen to Change the World

My wife was chosen to change the world, but for years she did not know it. The devil pointed out her fear, her insecurity and her feelings of rejection. "You can't do what your husband does! You just need to sit there." What is she doing now? She stands in front of a thousand prayer warriors and speaks into their lives. She decided she was going to do it even though she was afraid, even though she was insecure and did not want to face rejection.

My son Micah went through a time in his life when he did not want to be in the ministry. The enemy whispered, "Why should you go into the ministry? Your dad's traveling all over the place. How are you going to be bigger than your dad? You need to find something else to do." He got a marketing degree in college. Now he has completed a master's degree in theology—the Bible! He came to the realization that he was chosen to change the world. He gets calls from all over America, Australia and New Zealand to speak because he said yes.

Where would I be today if I had said no to God, or if I did not have a Bible? I was not raised in a Christian home, but before I was born, I was chosen to change the world. And I had the opportunity to make a decision for Christ forty-plus years ago. I have never been the same. If I would have said no, how many tens of thousands of people would not know the Lord today?

You Were Chosen to Change the World

What about you? Are you underestimating who you really are and what you can be? I mean, come on! Who wants to live eighty years on this planet and then go to heaven and only be able to say to God, "Well, I went to church every once in a while. I went to that men's thing and got a T-shirt. I gave occasionally."

You have been chosen. "Many are called, but few are chosen" (Matthew 22:14). Many are called. Many will read this book, but only a few will listen. I pray that you are one of a few who will realize that there is something in your life that you need to do for God. I hope you will realize that there is something that you must accomplish for God.

I did not wait to find the right people before I did something for God. I knew for myself that I was called to do something. God was so real to me that I had to touch people who had not been touched. People were hurting.

What would it be like if I secured a cure for cancer but kept it hidden for ten years? What would you feel if you found out that I had hidden the cure while cancer killed someone you loved? Your sister would have lived. Your brother would have lived. Your parent would have lived. "What is wrong with him?" you would say.

How about you? You have a cure. It is in your Bible. You have a cure for what you need. You have a cure for what everyone needs, regardless of the need. Your cure can remove sin and give someone purpose who had no purpose before. You have a cure. Would it be wrong to hold on to this cure for eighty years, never saying a word to anyone?

I want you to imagine a funeral. At the funeral, the pastor says, "He loved the Lord for sixty years." You turn to your neighbor and remark, "He was a Christian?! I didn't even know!" You have been chosen to change the world. You were not saved to sit in church. You have to go talk to people. The woman at the well was not in church (see John 4). The rich young ruler was not in church (see Mark 10). Nicodemus was not in church (see John 3). None of them were. They were all out there in the city. That is where you need to go!

Who is the lucky person who is going to run into you, the one chosen to change the world? Who is going to be in your path this week so that you can express the love of God to them and breathe life upon the person they are meant to be? Who is finally going to hear the truth because of an encounter with you? Who is going to know what it means for his or her life to change?

God says, "How much time do I need to give you? For how many years have I put you right where you are and given you an opportunity to do something?" Understand that you have been chosen to change the world. Understand that many hear but few believe. I want you to believe God. I want you to believe that you are able to turn a life on for Christ.

Quit waiting for some professional to come in and do what you are called to do. The bottom line is that you are not going to find a professional when you need one. God uses simple people like you and me who love Him and who go to church. He is going to use you—not your neighbor—to touch society. It is you. Wherever you go today, you are supposed to affect somebody. You are supposed to light up someone's day. I am serious!

2 | Fed Up, Filled Up and Fired Up

God is fed up with some things. Did you know that God can get fed up? He can. The Bible tells several stories of when God said, "Enough is enough!" Take a look at a few of them to see what I mean:

> The LORD observed the extent of human wickedness on the earth, and he saw that everything they thought or imagined was consistently and totally evil. So the LORD was sorry he had ever made them and put them on the earth. It broke his heart.
>
> Genesis 6:5–6

This was right before the flood. He got fed up.

> At dawn the next morning the angels became insistent. "Hurry," they said to Lot. "Take your wife and your two daughters who are here. Get out right now, or you will be swept away in the destruction of the city!" When Lot still

hesitated, the angels seized his hand and the hands of his wife and two daughters and rushed them to safety outside the city.

Genesis 19:15–16

This was right before the destruction of Sodom and Gomorrah. He got fed up. I believe God is fed up with some things that are going on in the world and in the Body of Christ. You see it. You know what I am talking about. The world is a mess, and the Church is not doing any better.

God is fed up. Are you?

I Am Fed Up

I am fed up with Christians being quiet when the world is dancing their sin down our streets. I am fed up that we do not have the backbone to stand up and say what we believe.

Cancel Culture and racism are causing people to wag their fingers at one another. We're not walking in love. We're looking to pick a fight.

I am fed up with lawlessness. I am fed up with law makers and the liberal media that gives teenagers the right to have an abortion but says it is wrong to pray in school.

I am fed up with school guidance counselors giving out free contraceptives for safe sex while never telling students that the best prevention method is to stay pure and remain a virgin. You know how we practiced safe sex in my day? We got married!

I am fed up with how one atheist can stop prayer in our schools, remove the Bible from schools and now wants to remove God from our United States Pledge of Allegiance. And Christians sit by apathetically because they do not want to deal with the blowback.

I am fed up with rappers, movies and men and women who shout foul language as easily as they breathe. I do not want my grandchildren to learn those words, and I am tired of hearing them on TV. I am tired of hearing people say them. Clean your mouth up!

I am fed up with humanistic, anti-Bible judges rewriting the meaning of marriage. God established what a proper marriage looks like, and it is between a man and a woman. Period.

I am fed up with fighting over defunding the police, puberty blockers, transgender material, sex education for elementary students and so many issues contrary to the Bible. We spend too much time in fantasyland and in other people's business—so much so that we are not getting any real Kingdom business done.

I am fed up with *The Bachelor* and *The Bachelorette* teaching this generation the wrong way to find a mate. And just so you know, 90 percent of the people who receive the last rose break up, so it does not work.

I am fed up with psychics. I am fed up with medium shows. I am fed up with hunting for ghosts. I am fed up with pet psychics. Do you realize there are pet psychics?!

"Here is my dog. Can you tell me what's wrong with him?"

"Yeah. I think he needs a bone."

"Thanks! Here's $100."

I am fed up with divorce and the passive way we deal with adultery and domestic abuse.

I am fed up that children have to raise their parents. Parents, it is time to grow up. It is time to lead your families and stop letting children lead themselves and us around.

I am fed up with boys acting like girls and girls acting like boys.

I am fed up with commercials using sex to sell every product, like Carl's Jr. using sex to sell a hamburger. I think Carl Jr. needs a spanking from Carl Sr.!

I am fed up with people getting stirred up and excited about spiritual things but not showing change. I am fed up with information but no transformation, and I am betting you would say, "Me, too."

God gets fed up when unrighteousness is on the rise. We should, too. It is fitting as His followers that we show an intolerance for what is contrary to His nature.

The Disciples Were Fed Up

The disciples were fed up. They were fed up with their fear. If you remember when Jesus died, they were hiding (see John 20:19). These men had walked with Jesus and had seen the miraculous up close. They had seen His power. Yet now they were hiding, and they got tired of it. They came to a point where they had to choose to either do or not do what Jesus said. Do you remember what He told them?

In Jesus' last message on this planet, five hundred people came together. It was the day of His ascension into glory. He said, "My brothers and sisters, I will be leaving now. What I want you to do is go to the Upper Room and wait for power from on high to come down. Wait there for this promise because while I can only be in one city in the physical, the Holy Spirit can be in all cities at all times."[1]

And then Jesus started floating up. That is a great close to a message! If I could do that, you would be impressed.

After witnessing all of that, you would think everyone there would say, "We must go to the Upper Room! The Man just told us what to do and then floated off to heaven!" But that is not what happened. Really, only 120 disciples out of the 500 ended up going to the Upper Room. The 380 who did not go were never heard of again in the Bible.

I want you to hear me: There is going to be an opportunity for you to go to your own Upper Room and get exactly what the disciples got two thousand years ago. And what is exciting is that it is going to be the greatest night of your life. The disciples were sick of their fear. They were fed up with where they were. And when you get fed up, you get filled up.

Filled Up

Let me show you this in Acts 1:8. It says, "You will receive power when the Holy Spirit comes upon you." You are going to receive something. It is not just speaking in tongues, although many believe that accompanies it. There is power connected to what you will receive. The power for what? The power to help you live the kind of life God wants you to live. The power to be able to fight an enemy who is stronger than you. This infilling will give you power.

You must understand that the devil is a terrorist. You cannot negotiate with terrorists, right? We live in a day when terrorists do not hide. They blow people up and want you to know it was them. That is the way the devil is. You are going to need Holy Spirit power. Do not leave your Upper Room without the power. You must have it so that you can become all God wants you to be.

Years ago, I spoke at Planetshakers, which is a global movement aimed at equipping generations to reach the world. I have known its founders, Russell and Sam Evans, for over twenty years. I have a huge love for Australia and have spoken there many times. On this occasion, I was speaking in Melbourne.

I was on the platform preaching a message, and I was only about halfway through when I felt led to illustrate how we are to take the devil down. In this illustration, I walk from the back of the stage and re-create Jesus dominating Satan as He went down to hell and defeated death, hell and the grave. As I portray myself as Jesus, I soundly beat and dominate Satan.

When I gave this illustration, everyone in attendance jumped to their feet and began to roar. The sound man said it went to 122 decibels in the room. The sound level was loud enough to burst eardrums, but the crowd did not realize it because the energy in the room was so intense. And that sound did not last for twenty seconds; it went on for twenty minutes. There was breakthrough. It was not my preaching—it was the sound of a group of people who were mobilized in unison. Their spirits were in one accord with one goal. It was a pivotal moment I will never forget.

It is not about whether or not our church services are good, or if we sing really well during worship or if we are really loud. There is something in the spiritual realm that we wake up when we are so fed up with the state of this world and our pitiful lives that we want to get filled up with power to make a difference. When you get a mindset to do that, you will have revival. Your community will have revival. Your state and your nation will have revival! But it starts with you.

Fired Up

In the Upper Room, the disciples waited for the filling of the Holy Spirit. There was not clever preaching going on. There was not a flow of persuasive or inspiring words. They waited prayerfully, expectantly, for the Holy Spirit's arrival. Suddenly, there was a sound. The Bible tells us it was similar to a roaring windstorm, and this windstorm filled the room (see Acts 2:1–2). Then the Holy Spirit fell upon the disciples.

Before the Holy Spirit fell and before the disciples spoke in tongues, the atmosphere in the house had changed. I want you to see this. They did not get the Holy Spirit first and then the house changed. The atmosphere in the house changed, and then they were filled with the Holy Spirit. So the atmosphere has the ability to bring the Spirit of God to you.

The Bible says the house shook. The Holy Spirit entered, and the house shook. Do you realize that what happened then can happen now? If it happened then, it can happen again. Often when we read the Bible, we read it as if it were a fictional story in which something happens just one time. No. When God enters the building, the building shakes.

Then the disciples were filled up with the Holy Spirit. *Then* they preached the Word of God with boldness. Where there is boldness, there is no fear. If you have fear in your life, you probably do not have the Holy Spirit.

THE ATMOSPHERE IN THE HOUSE CHANGED, AND THEN THEY WERE FILLED WITH THE HOLY SPIRIT.

I have worked very hard at being bold when it comes to sharing my faith. I have no problem talking to anybody. It is easy. It does not matter who they are. I am able to find a spot where we can talk, and I will end up praying for them and they will get saved. If I can cheer radically for a sports team, then I can talk loudly and boldly for my Lord. I need even more passion to share Jesus. Being bold to share the Gospel message takes courage. That is my bold mentality as I go about my day.

You must have this boldness in your life. Ananias had that boldness when he went to Saul (before he was renamed Paul).

He told him, "Brother Saul, the Lord Jesus, who appeared to you on the road, has sent me so that you might regain your sight and be filled with the Holy Spirit" (Acts 9:17). Saul was blind when Ananias showed up, but not for long. The Holy Spirit is attached to the miraculous, and as Saul regained his sight, he also gained an infilling. Our world desperately wants to see the miraculous in the Church and in our lives. They come looking, but they do not see the power of God. It is about time we get out there and ask God to dump this power on us.

Later when Saul was renamed Paul and filled with the Holy Spirit, he looked a sorcerer in the eye (see Acts 13:9). Really, he looked the devil in the eye that day.

I Want It! I Need It!

Let me tell you a funny story. I got saved while I was playing college football. It was my senior year, and the movie *The Exorcist* had just come out. That movie terrified a lot of the football players—grown men had to sleep with the lights on because this movie was so realistic. I went to a church service after I got saved, and they wanted to pray for me to receive the Holy Spirit. I did not know what that was, so I said, "I can't handle any more of God right now. I just got saved!"

That weekend I went to a Pentecostal church and was asked to play the guitar. I had never heard a Christian song, but they thought I would pick them up quickly because I played by ear. They sang several songs: "Oh, the Blood of Jesus," "Nothing but the Blood of Jesus," and "There Is Power in the Blood." That is when I started thinking that I might have joined a vampire cult! This was the bloodiest song service I had ever been in.

After the time of ministry, they asked me to help pray for people to receive the Holy Spirit. Remember, I just got saved. I am not filled. I do not even own a Bible. But they told me to lay my hands on people's heads and they would get it. I asked what they would get, and my friend Denny said, "You'll see!"

I went over to a guy who looked as if he was around 28 years old. He was down on his knees shaking. I looked at him and figured that he had a nerve problem and needed to go to the hospital, but I asked him what he wanted. He said, "I want the Holy Spirit." I told him to hang on, and I asked Denny what to do. He said to put my hand on his head and ask God to fill him. When I did, the Lord filled him, and suddenly he began speaking in tongues. I jumped out of my skin! *What happened to him? He will never be able to keep a job now! He cannot talk English anymore!*

After that, Denny told me to go pray for a lady. She also received the infilling of the Holy Spirit. Then Denny began to teach about how much we need the Holy Spirit to live and how He was a gift from God.

Now, honestly, did you not just lean in the first time you heard someone speaking in tongues and listen to see if there was a word in English in there? Like, what are they saying? "Skin-of-my-knee?" "Come-tie-my-bowtie?" As I was watching those two speak in tongues, I realized, *Wow, I want that! I need that! If it is a gift from God, I want to open it!* So I ran over to Danny while he was preaching and stuck his hand on my head. He asked, "What are you doing?" I said, "Do me! Do me now! I want the Holy Spirit now. I want the gift from God!" I was filled that night.

Being filled up with the Holy Spirit gave me the power to take a hard stand for what I believe, to speak into the lives of others, to see change in their lives, to see sickness and disease disappear and to send demons packing. I knew very little about the Bible in my early days, but I had God's name and the Holy Spirit's power. You can, too!

You do not need to have a seminary degree to live in a state of revival. You do not have to understand the process from start to finish. All you need is to get fed up with where you are right now, to desire something better and to go after it until you are filled with the Holy Spirit. Are you fed up? Great! That is step one. Let's get moving. The same Spirit that came upon the disciples wants to fill you, too. Open your heart to receive all that He has for you. Only then will you be fired up to do the will of God, to change the world.

3 | Are You Heart-Healthy?

Life and death are in the power of the tongue. That is biblical. "The tongue can bring death or life; those who love to talk will reap the consequences" (Proverbs 18:21). Consequences can be painful. The verse before says that "Wise words satisfy like a good meal" (verse 20). They fill a person up. We see from these two verses that the quality of our lives depends upon the words that we use.

God created the universe by the power of the spoken word. Jesus set us free by the power of the spoken word. We are saved by the power of our spoken word. We can word-bless people or word-curse people. I am not talking about profanity as much as speaking critically to a person: being negative, belittling, being judgmental, accusing or blaming. When you talk to somebody in this way, God calls it corrupt communication (see Ephesians 4:29–32).

You are empowering them to fail when you word-curse them.

Oppositely, you can empower the people around you to prosper by blessing them with your mouth. You can edify

A Heart on Fire

and encourage them. You can build them up and praise them. You can restore them with your words. The Bible says our words are that powerful, and they are eternal (see Matthew 12:36; Psalm 119:89).

Do you bless people with your words? Do you empower them to prosper? "Whatever is in your heart determines what you say" (Matthew 12:34). So if you have a mouth problem, you have a heart problem because the Bible says you speak out of the abundance, or fullness, of your heart.

A Mouth Problem Is a Heart Problem

Our words are important, and what we dwell on is important, too. That is why David, the psalmist, said, "May the words of my mouth and the meditation of my heart be pleasing to you, O LORD, my rock and my redeemer" (Psalm 19:14). Your heart and your mouth are connected.

My words have power. They are keys to unlocking and releasing the pain in the hearts of others. My words can protect a heart from wounding, pain, hardness and spiritual deadness. My words can breathe life into broken places if I will use them. The same is true for your words. Your words have power. They can unlock, release, protect and restore. You just have to use them. You have to be aware of when to speak, what to speak and when to remain silent.

Do You Have a Heart Problem?

What is the condition of your spiritual heart?

In the natural, you can have a heart condition and just drop dead. It can be fatal. Everybody knows that. But did you know you can also have a fatal spiritual heart condition?

44

The heart is a muscular organ that pumps blood throughout your entire body. It is also the central or the innermost part of your being. Your heart is your spirit man. Your heart is where the Holy Spirit resides at the point of salvation. "For with the heart a person believes, resulting in righteousness, and with the mouth he confesses, resulting in salvation" (Romans 10:10 NASB). You need your heart to be able to believe in Jesus.

Your heart is the seat of your emotions. It is where your motives, thoughts, intentions and desires reside. The state of your heart is the state of your life. "You must love the LORD your God with all your heart, all your soul, and all your mind" (Matthew 22:37). Luke says almost exactly the same thing: "All your heart, all your soul, all your strength, and all your mind" (Luke 10:27). That is how you are to love the Lord your God.

A Surprise Heart Problem

June 5, 2009 was a rough day for me. I went to the doctor because I was having pain in my left hand that ran up to my neck. They sent me home with heartburn medicine. On the way home, I swung by the grocery store and picked up some chips and Häagen-Dazs ice cream, which I no longer eat. I bought chips and ice cream because I wanted to celebrate. There I was, sitting on the couch and eating my ice cream and chips. I was so happy.

My wife was at church teaching a class that night. She got home about eight thirty. About an hour or so later, I began to have really strong chest pains. We jumped in the car, drove ninety miles an hour and got to the emergency room as fast as we could. Thank God for the Holy Spirit watching over me. I should have had a massive heart attack. Doctors and medical personnel who looked at my records asked, "Did this person make it?" I had three 95 percent blockages and one 80 percent blockage in my heart.

Someone can have a massive heart attack and die with just one blockage. I had four blockages. And the miracle of the day was that I did not even really have a heart attack. I was starting to have one when we reached the emergency room. Also, there were no other patients in the emergency room. The staff watched me all night. I had the enzyme in my blood that showed that I was having a heart attack, but it never escalated to heart attack level. It was, however, very, very serious—and I did not even know I had a heart problem!

I do not want you to have a surprise spiritual heart attack today, so let's examine one way in which your heart can be spiritually sick.

A Sin of the Heart and the Mouth

In my years of pastoring, there is one particular sin that I saw that connected the heart and the mouth time and time again. It is the sin of unforgiveness. Someone did something to you, and you cannot let it go. Maybe something unjust was done, and there is a good reason you feel the way you do. Your heart is wounded, and you are bleeding out through the thoughts you think and the words you say. You are bleeding on everybody.

Blood attracts sharks, right? In the spirit, blood attracts demons. You do not want that. You do not want your wounds to attract the enemy because where he is, more problems will exist. You want to cauterize that wound as fast as possible to stop the bleeding. You want to dress the wound, wash it daily and be healed of it. You want to be whole again.

Unforgiveness is a sin of the heart and the mouth. Consider Matthew 18:23–35. In this passage, Jesus tells us that the Kingdom of heaven is like a king who wanted to settle accounts with his servants. One of his servants owed him the equivalent of millions of dollars—something he could not repay. The servant fell on his knees and begged for the king to have patience. He promised that everything would be repaid. The king's heart was moved with compassion, and he released the servant from his debts. He canceled the debt. He forgave him.

The story goes on to say that the servant went out immediately to find a guy who owed him roughly twenty dollars. He caught the man by the throat and threatened, "Pay what you owe me!" The man begged, just as the servant had, for patience, but he did not get it. He was put in prison until he could pay the debt. No mercy. No forgiveness.

The king heard about the wicked servant's behavior and called for him to come to the king. He said, "You contemptible, wicked servant! I forgave you! I canceled your great debt because you begged me. But you had no pity for your fellow man and threw him in prison." Then, the king called for the jailers and had the servant turned over to the torturers until he could pay all that he owed. Jesus ended this teaching saying, "That's what my heavenly Father will do to you if you refuse to forgive your brothers and sisters from your heart" (Matthew 18:35).

Let me tell you, this is a powerful word. If we do not forgive others their sins and trespasses, God will not forgive us. We will suffer many wounds. God will turn us over to the tormentors, the demons. You do not want to be turned over by our heavenly Father. If you are turned over, you are not saved. I believe we have missed how important this is in the Body of Christ. Yes, we suffer many wounds in this life. The Lord knows it. We get hurt in our marriages. We get hurt by our children. We get hurt in our churches. Often, we do not make it out of childhood without wounds. These bleeding wounds cause sicknesses. They cause divorces. They cause problems in the Church.

When you choose not to forgive, when you determine that you are going to hold an offense, you begin to die spiritually. That is what the Bible says (see Proverbs 18:21). But I am writing to speak life to you, to speak freedom and healing to you so that you will not be lost in spiritual darkness.

Maybe you did not know it when you got up this morning, but today is your day. Child of God, Jesus was sent to pay the huge debt that we could not pay. It was far more than millions or even billions of dollars. It cost Him His perfect life. Even though it cost Him, Jesus paid the debt for us. Knowing that, how is it that we cannot forgive others their little offenses? God is forgiving us every day for our great offenses. Matthew 6:15 in the Amplified Translation says, "If you do not forgive others [nurturing your hurt and anger with the result that it interferes with your relationship with God], then your Father will not forgive your trespasses." It is very clear.

Three Main Causes of Unforgiveness

There are three main causes of unforgiveness: spiritual immaturity, taking offense and a flesh that has not been crucified. Hurt is going to come in this life. Everyone is going to be hurt at one time or another. But how we deal with people or situations that hurt us is what determines if we will find our hearts infected with unforgiveness.

Spiritual immaturity. Mature Christians will not harbor unforgiveness in their heart. They know unforgiveness is poison to their soul. In maturity, they watch their words. They change their words to bless and empower others to prosper. Immature believers empower others to fail by lashing out with pain in their hearts.

"Understand this, my dear brothers and sisters: You must all be quick to listen, slow to speak, and slow to get angry" (James 1:19). You cannot become offended. You cannot carry unforgiveness. You cannot have a wounded heart. You cannot be spiritually immature and do the will of God. God is counting on you, and if you are carrying unforgiveness, you cannot be counted on. You are spiritually immature.

When we step into maturity and begin to watch the words that come out of our mouths, we do less hurting. We do less wounding. We do less offending, and we offer healing instead. We offer hope. We speak life to those around us, and they thrive as a result.

Offense. Offense reveals your heart. Being easily offended is a sign that we are living in the last days. Jesus says many will be offended (see Matthew 24:10–12). But you know what? I do not want to be part of that statistic. That is why I refuse to be offendable. You have to do that to protect yourself from the sin of unforgiveness. You must grow up, child of God. Grow up. Realize that offense is from the pit of hell. Offense is not something you want to harbor.

You get offended at home. You get offended at church. You get offended at your workplace. Wherever you go, whomever you come in contact with, you get offended. But the Bible tells us, "Great peace have they which love thy law: and nothing shall offend them" (Psalm 119:165 KJV). Spiritually mature people who know the Word of God want to live it. They want to have a life of abundance, victory and peace. They will be unoffendable.

At some point we are all offended by a word or deed. I do not know one person who has never been offended. I also do not know anyone who has never offended someone else. We must learn to deal with offense. We must learn how to shake it off.

I meet people all the time who want to be used by God. They want to be warriors on the front line, but they are offended. They are Davids; they are Deborahs. They could do so much for the Kingdom of God, but they are offended. God cannot count on them to walk the road before them with maturity.

Maybe your offense feels justified. Maybe someone hurt you. They abused you and did all sorts of bad things to you. Yes, what they did was wrong. Your offense is justifiable, but that does not make it okay to live offended or to make room for unforgiveness in your heart. You cannot afford to carry it. It is too much for you. It will crush you. You have got to release it. You have got to give it to God. You have got to say, "I choose not to be offended. I choose to be a mature child of the Most High God."

Offense hurts—a lot. Sometimes it comes at you from all directions. Sometimes it is a test, and sometimes the enemy uses the people closest to you to tear you down. He uses your husband or wife, your children, your friend or your coworker. Regardless of how or why it happens, we have to grow up in the Body of Christ or we are going to be put in prison. If we refuse to forgive from the heart, we are going to be put in prison by the heavenly Father (see Matthew 18:34–35).

We must forgive. Jesus was sent to be tortured and die on a cross to ensure the payment of mankind's sins. Since our debt has been released, we should release others of their debts to us as well. We must walk in forgiveness.

A flesh that has not been crucified. Did you know that in the Christian walk we are to die to self? The Bible tells us that those who belong to Christ have crucified the passions and desires of their sinful selves to the cross (see Galatians 5:24). If you were dead to self, you would not feel the sting when others say hurtful words to you. But the fact that their words pierce you deeply tells you that your flesh is still very much alive. We must crucify our flesh. You want a Scripture for that? "If you refuse to take up your cross and follow me, you are not worthy of being mine" (Matthew 10:38). Wow. What do you think about that?

Take up your cross and follow Jesus. Die daily. Your flesh needs to die. God has called you to be a warrior, and the only way you can be trusted on the battlefield is by the maturity you show in training. Mature believers refuse to walk in unforgiveness. They refuse to allow their flesh to rule them.

Seven Consequences

As I said before, there are consequences for the words that you speak. Either you will bring life or you will bring death by the words of your mouth. Here are seven consequences you should know that come from the sin of unforgiveness. If you receive what I am about to tell you, it will change your life forever.

1. Unforgiveness hardens your heart. You wonder why you have not been able to feel God. I am telling you right now, it is because there is unforgiveness in your heart, and that is sin.

It separates you from God. If you do not forgive immediately, your heart begins to harden. A hardened heart cannot feel the presence of God. It cannot perceive or feel God. It cannot hear the voice of God.

A HARDENED HEART CANNOT FEEL THE PRESENCE OF GOD.

You say, "I am justified in my offense!" You might be justified. But do you desire the presence of God? Do you love His presence? If you love the presence of God, you will pay the price. You will do whatever it takes to have access to Him. Your heart will cry out, "Don't take Your presence from me. That hurtful person is Your problem. Those hurtful words, that hurtful deed—I am going to give them to You, God, because I want Your presence in my life."

Sin comes to separate you from God. A wounded heart will prevent you from feeling God. Guard your heart and refuse unforgiveness entrance to it.

2. Unforgiveness contaminates your anointing. You can still minister under the anointing God has given you, but it will not be a pure anointing if you are harboring unforgiveness. It will be a contaminated anointing. If you are in ministry, things that are off base will leak into what you speak from your heart. Your worship will have a wounded vibe. I do not want that for you. I want you to have a pure anointing and pure motives because the purer your heart becomes, the stronger your anointing will be.

3. Unforgiveness wounds your heart. Listen to me: This is very important. You will be hurt and disappointed in others at some point in this life. If you choose to become offended, to walk in unforgiveness, you will remain wounded. You will keep bleeding. You will attract demons. You will open doors to the enemy. You will give the enemy access to you, to attack your physical body, to trouble your mind, to send you into despair. It is all connected: body, soul and spirit. Even your ability to sleep is affected by your ability to forgive others. I have seen it happen to people around me. When they were finally able to forgive after years and years of holding an offense, they went to bed and slept soundly for hours. God wants you, His beloved, to sleep well. He wants you to have divine health. You just have to allow Him to cauterize your wound and stop the bleeding. That is how you will receive it.

4. You will become the thing you will not forgive. You conform to pain, sickness and bitterness. You become sick and start to claim your sickness: "my" cancer, "my" unforgiveness, "my" bitterness, "my" arthritis.

You become the thing you will not forgive. It becomes an excuse not to function in the Body of Christ. You say, "I don't want to do anything in that church. They hurt me one time, so I'm not going to get involved." It becomes an excuse not to serve God. You use your pain to excuse yourself. Grow up, child of God. It is time to become spiritually mature and release those who wronged you. Release that pastor. Release that ex-husband. It is not worth holding on to the pain.

I remember a lady who came up to me after service one day and said, "My husband, who died ten years ago, did this, this, this and this to me."

I asked, "He's dead?"

"Yes. He died ten years ago."

"And you're still hurting about what he did to you?"

That is how long we can carry things. We can carry pain for a lifetime. Who can heal a broken, wounded heart? Not time—only Jesus.

5. Unforgiveness closes the heavens above you. "If you refuse to forgive others, your Father will not forgive your sins" (Matthew 6:15). The heavens are closed to you. I do not know of anybody who can afford a closed heaven. God is my Source. I take comfort in knowing that I can go to my Father, and I go to my Father frequently. If my conversation is all about what someone did to me, I am focusing more on them than I am on God. I want my words to be, "It doesn't matter what they did. I release them to You, Father."

6. Unforgiveness locks you in your past. You cannot speak or live in the now of God when you are still talking about your mother abandoning you, your spouse verbally abusing you, your friend betraying you or your child disowning you. Get out of your past. Do not get locked in. If you keep staring backward, you will not have the now blessings of God. Your focus is on your wound, your energy is wrapped up in unforgiveness and your words drip with pain. Remember, out of the abundance of the heart the mouth speaks. Let God heal your heart today.

7. Unforgiveness causes you to become spiritually stagnant. When you are stagnant, you cannot move in rhythm with the Holy Spirit. You cannot advance in your relationship with God because you are stuck. You cannot advance in your relationship with your wife, your husband, your children or others you love because you are offended. You are offended at the church and cannot feel the presence of God anymore. Your emotions are sealed off. Child of God, you have to decide if it is going to be God's way or your way. Are you going to stagnate because you want to hold a grudge, or are you going to release the ones who hurt you and free yourself for a shower of refreshing?

I wish you would say, "It's Your way, Lord. It's Your Kingdom. You paid for my sin. It was a debt I could have never paid. Had it not been for You, I would have no hope. It's the least I can do to forgive my brother or sister, husband or wife, child, friend or church member of their sin. I release my hurt today. I don't want to be stuck in the past when I can live in the now of God and move in rhythm with the Holy Spirit."

I am asking you to examine yourself today. Unforgiveness may be why you are not advancing. It may be why you are not experiencing revival, or why you are not on fire for the things of God.

Whom do you need to release? You may have thought you had completely forgiven them, but be open and honest with God. Just make sure you cover that base. Say their name out loud. Do not just think it. Just like you could not think the salvation prayer, you have to speak some things out. Do not commit a sin of silence. If you keep quiet about it, if you do not confess it and give it to the Lord, then nothing is going to change.

Right now, the Holy Spirit is reaching out to you. He is saying, "Today is the day for you to become unstuck, to get rid of the offense, to release the hurt." You say that the person who hurt you does not deserve to be forgiven, but let me tell you, it is not worth the pain to hold on to that offense. Just let it go. Begin to speak it out, saying, "I release it. I choose to forgive. God, help me release it. Heal my heart."

I want you to be spiritually mature today and realize that you have to shake off the sin of unforgiveness. You must come out of your pain, come out of your woundedness. Forgive. Release. Do not allow your heart to become encrusted. Do not get stuck in the past. Do not foster your wounds. Be healthy and whole. God has something better for you than what you have ever experienced. God has something new for you, and it starts with Him healing your heart. Let the Lord heal you.

God feels your pain. He says, "Enough is enough!" His love is enough. Forgive others. Forgive yourself. Be free.

Peter came to Jesus and asked, "Lord, how often should I forgive someone who sins against me?" (Matthew 18:21). And if you study Peter, you discover he had a kind of foot-shaped mouth. He was always sticking his foot in his mouth. This time was no different. He was asking a question with a number already in his mind.

He was probably thinking, *How often should you forgive people? Two times? No, I don't want to say that because that is kind of low. How about four times? Four would be a lot. That would take a lot to forgive. No, I'm going to really go overboard with it. I'm going to ask if seven times is enough!*

Jesus replied to Peter's question about whether forgiving seven times is enough, "No, not seven times, but seventy times seven!" (see verse 22). It is as if Jesus was saying, "You want to use sevens? Let's just go with sevens then!" It is not that we only have to forgive seventy times seven. That number represents an immeasurable amount. Who is really going to count that high?

Jesus purchased our freedom and forgave our sins. "For he has rescued us from the kingdom of darkness and transferred us into the Kingdom of his dear Son, who purchased our freedom and forgave our sins" (Colossians 1:13–14). I am free because of Jesus. You are free because of Jesus. Maybe you do not know if you are right with God, but you can get right with Him. He is standing ready to forgive you, to set you free from your past and to heal you from your hurt.

Put your hand over your heart and pray:

Father God, I choose not to be offended. I choose to forgive. Forgive me, Lord, for holding offense toward

You. I am sorry. You are a good God. Forgive me. I choose to release my mother, father, husband, wife, ex-husband, ex-wife, brother, sister, friend, pastor and church member. I release them all. I cannot carry the offense any longer. I do not want it in my life. I renounce bitterness. I renounce anger. I renounce unforgiveness in the name of Jesus. Lord, do surgery on my heart today. I take authority now, and I break every power of darkness that has come because of the offense. I break the power of unforgiveness and bitterness, and I command every chain be loosed in the name of Jesus. Lord Jesus, thank You for purchasing my freedom. I do not deserve it, but You love me so much. Forgive me of my sins and all my unrighteousness. Forgive all the mistakes I have made, all the bad things I have done, all the people I have hurt, and even forgive those who have hurt me. You are such a good God! In Jesus' name, Amen.

4 | Developing a Heart Receptive to Revival

My wife, Deborah, and I burn for revival. Our hearts have been passionately pursuing God for many years, and nothing is as exciting as seeing men and women who are spiritually set on fire to know Him more. It is this desire that causes our hearts to burn.

One day, Deborah spoke to God and said, "Lord, do You know what? We have prayed for revival for so many years. I mean, I don't know if we can keep on praying and not see it happen. We must be doing something wrong. I feel as if You want to send revival and You're waiting on us. But we're waiting on You, while You're still waiting on us. So this is what we're going to do. We're going to declare revival. We will tell the people that Monday night is revival night."

Deborah is an open book. She tells it like she sees it, and she gets excited over things. Well, after she prayed, she got excited. That Sunday, Deborah got up in front of the church and told everybody that Monday night was going to be revival night. She shared what revival night meant to her and that we were going to pray for everyone, even if it cost us staying at the church until nine or ten o'clock at night. I do not think she anticipated how less than enthusiastic some of our church members were going to be about the idea of a Monday night service. But whatever it meant, we were going to the next level. Revival always has to be birthed, and anything that has to be birthed must be bathed in prayer.

This went on for some time. With an innocent heart, she got up on stage before our church every weekend and reminded them about the service on Monday. She was sure they wanted revival as much as we did. Then, during a Sunday afternoon prayer meeting with some friends, she received some words from the Lord that were not positive about the condition of the people's hearts. I will just leave it at that.

Faithful as ever, Deborah showed up Monday night. She was opening the service when she had a sudden realization—and it was not a good one! And because she is an open book, she shared it in the microphone. That "suddenly" went all over the city. It was on livestream. It was in front of everybody. Word gets around. You are curious now, right? You want to know what her "suddenly" was? It was this: the people do not want revival.

Not everyone will be as excited about or as invested in seeing revival as you may be. Not everyone will buy a book on revival in the hopes that it will bring them one step closer to experiencing it in their lives. Not everyone will set aside time to pray for a personal revival, let alone gather corporately to pray for revival to come to their church or city. This is why you do not see many church-wide or even regional revivals. But listen, do not let someone else's lack of passion stop you from experiencing all that God has for you. God can birth revival in your life without the participation of anyone but you.

Complacency Breeds Complacency

Deborah realized that night, standing before our people, that she wanted revival at any cost, that I wanted revival at any cost, but our people did not want revival at any cost. Suddenly she felt like a mother. It is reasonable for a mother to burp her baby and change its diapers, but it is unreasonable for a mother to do the same when the "baby" is ten years old.

She spoke in the microphone, "I'm tired of nursing you all. I'm tired of changing your diapers. I can't do this. I'm tired! I can't drag your dead weight. I don't need to talk tonight." She handed over the microphone to one of our pastors and went home.

I had just gotten back from a meeting in Australia, and I was watching the whole thing via livestream. When she walked into the house, all I said was, "How was prayer meeting?"

She responded, "Well, if you want to know the truth, it was really horrible. I mean, it didn't turn out horribly, but it was horrible for me."

I told her what I felt in my spirit. "It was God."

It was God. They needed to hear her rebuke. They needed a wake-up call.

The next morning God spoke very clearly to Deborah. "Complacency breeds complacency." God was turning something inside Deborah. She had gotten to the place that whatever He wanted her to do, she was determined to see this revival birthed. And that is how our city meeting started. Something is shifting even today in the atmosphere over Modesto, California, because of it. Revival is coming!

We Cannot Be Satisfied Where We Are

Each one of us needs to get to the same place that Deborah did. We need to fall down before God and say, "Whatever You want me to do, Lord, I will do it. I need to see Your revival birthed in me."

You cannot let excuses get in the way. You have to plan to spend time in prayer. You have to plan to spend time in the Word. You have to plan to sit in the presence of God. You have to plan for it, or it will never happen. You have to develop an expectation and faith that God will meet you in those moments that you set aside with Him.

To be complacent means to be satisfied with where you are presently. Complacency is not a good word for Christians. Contentment with godliness is great gain, but complacency, being satisfied with where you are, is not how we were designed to live. We are never to stop growing. God moves us from glory to glory. There is never any transformation without personal pain.

Complacency is the same as religion. Religion is manmade. It is dull, lifeless, mechanical and legalistic. It is having a form of godliness but denying its power (see 2 Timothy 3:5). The Holy Spirit is power, and this gift was given to us by Jesus at Pentecost to live and breathe inside us.

Christianity is not a religion—it is a relationship. It is a Father-son relationship. It is a Father-daughter relationship. It is a love relationship. He adopted you, and that is why you can cry out to Him, "Abba, Father" (Romans 8:15). He loves you, and He is after your heart.

God Is After Your Heart

God is after your heart. You can go to church, hear your pastor's message, put your hand on your heart, pray a prayer—even mean it! But on most weeks, you return home, and within a few days the enemy comes, persecution and trials come, and your seed of faith is stolen. You find you are right back in the same rut. Why does that happen? Because your heart does not fully belong to God. There are parts of it that you have not surrendered to Him.

> **THERE IS NEVER ANY TRANSFORMATION WITHOUT PERSONAL PAIN.**

Your heart is hardened. It is wounded. It is offended. It is complacent. This is why you cannot retain the Word. You are responsible for it and responsible for your lack of surrender. Thank God that today is your day to do something about it!

When you surrender your heart completely to God, when you let Him into the parts that you have denied exist and have kept locked up, your heart will soften. You will repent and change your behavior. And suddenly you will notice you are accelerating spiritually. This is the proper position for revival.

Do you want spiritual acceleration? For God to transform your life, you must first surrender. You must die to your will and way of doing things. "My old self has been crucified with Christ. It is no longer I who live, but Christ lives in me. So I live in this earthly body by trusting in the Son of God, who loved me and gave himself for me" (Galatians 2:20). What does God want you to die to? Jesus didn't come to hurt you; He came to "kill you." He wants you to die to sin, selfishness, rebellion, pride and anger.

Jesus said to His disciples, "If any of you wants to be my follower, you must give up your own way, take up your cross, and follow me" (Matthew 16:24). That does not sound as if we can casually say a prayer or hear a message and then forget about it and go about our lives. It sounds to me like we pick up our cross, deny ourselves daily and say, "God, what is my assignment today? I am absolutely surrendered. I am all in. My energy is Yours. My time is Yours. My talent is Yours. My finances are Yours." If God does not have all of you, you have a problem. But when He has all of you, He will do miraculous things in and through you!

When my wife and I moved our family two thousand miles from Louisiana to California, it felt as if we were moving to a different country. Everything was so different! We had to die to what home had felt like to us. We had to pick up our cross and die so that we could live for Jesus and see people saved in California—so that we could see revival. That is what we did for Jesus. It was His will, not our will. It took several years, but Modesto became our home. It became our place of blessing.

God wants your heart, your opinions, your reasoning and your complacency. He wants your pride, ego and selfishness to die. He wants absolute surrender. You can surrender more. I know because I am still surrendering more and more to Him. I thought maybe I had surrendered everything, but there is always more to give.

Sin is what prevents us from giving everything to God. One of those sins that we talked about in the last chapter is unforgiveness. It can be the condition of our heart in response to this journey called life. Sometimes people do things to you that wound your heart. Sometimes you wound yourself. Either way, we must be aware of the condition of our heart and do the hard work of keeping it tender before God.

The state of your heart is the state of your life. That is why there are more than seven hundred passages in the Bible that relate to the heart. Both God and Satan are after your heart. One will win, and you get to choose who. "Guard your heart above all else, for it determines the course of your life" (Proverbs 4:23).

What is the heart, beyond the organ beating in our chest? The heart represents the innermost part of your being, and it is where the Holy Spirit resides. The heart is where your attitudes, motives, thoughts, intentions and desires originate. So let's talk about four heart conditions: the lukewarm heart, the wounded heart, the hardened heart and the broken heart. The condition of your heart determines what God is able to do in and through you. That is why it is very important that we know about these dominant heart conditions and what to look for when we are self-assessing so that we can determine if we are where we need to be for God to move in us.

The Lukewarm Heart

The Bible tells us, "I know all the things you do, that you are neither hot nor cold. I wish that you were one or the other! But since you are like lukewarm water, neither hot nor cold, I will spit you out of my mouth!" (Revelation 3:15–16). Wow. God is saying that He will vomit out of His mouth anyone who straddles the fence in his or her Christianity. Clearly, God does not like lukewarm. He would rather you be cold. He would much rather you be hot, of course, but the Bible says He would rather you be cold than lukewarm.

We must consider what a strong statement that is. I think we cannot just whitewash that and cover it over, saying, "But God understands my life. He understands how hard everything is and how I have to make a living and how I do not have time for Him." Let's get something straight: He hates lukewarm. He would rather you be cold.

"Don't store up treasures here on earth, where moths eat them and rust destroys them, and where thieves break in and steal. Store your treasures in heaven, where moths and rust cannot destroy, and thieves do not break in and steal. Wherever your treasure is, there the desires of your heart will also be."

Matthew 6:19–21

Where is your heart?

If you have a mouth problem, you have a heart problem.

If you love shopping more than you love God . . .

If you love fishing more than you love God . . .

If you love eating more than you love God . . .

If you love your significant other more than you love God . . .

If you love anything more than you love God, that is where your heart is going to be. That is your treasure.

If it is golf you love, you will be on the golf course.

If it is fishing you love, you will be on the lake.

If it is shopping you love, you will be at the mall.

If it is eating you love, you will be at the restaurant.

None of those things is horrible in and of itself, but what the Lord is trying to get through to you is that if we love anything more than we love Him, His presence, His Word and His Church, then God does not have all of our heart. If God is not Lord of all, He is not Lord at all. It is plain and clear.

Do you have a lukewarm heart? Have you lost your first love? In the past I had. So has my wife. She tells others that in the early years of our marriage, she put me in the place of God. But it was not long before she realized she needed God more than ever as a married woman.

Jesus must be everything. He must be your Savior, Friend, Deliverer, Confidant—everything. His presence must be what you desire. When it is not and you push Him to the back burner, you have lost your first love. You have developed a fatal heart condition. Lukewarmness is fatal for your spirit man.

One of the most important things in your life is spending time with God. My wife tells the story of how she prayed continuously for two years for God to give her back her first love. She had grown apathetic, and it grieved her. He gave it back to her during a time of trouble, and she was changed. She was better equipped to handle the difficulties she faced because she knew with everything inside of her that she loved Jesus more than anything else in her life. She knew that He would surround her with peace to get through all the trials and pain that life was throwing our way.

When you have more of God and less of yourself, God will manifest His presence through you. When you go into a room, the atmosphere of the room will change. You manifest His presence. You are a fire for Him.

Do not give in to lukewarm Christianity. Keep moving forward. You cannot stand still with God. He is a God of forward motion, not a God of standing still or sliding backward.

The eyes of the Lord search the whole earth looking for those who are fully committed to Him, to strengthen them and show His might on their behalf (see 2 Chronicles 16:9). If it seems as though God has not been strong for you, if it seems as if nothing changes when you (with God) enter a situation, you need to ask yourself if your heart is completely His. Is He first place in your life, or is your heart lukewarm?

You can make a new commitment with your head, but it will not do any good if your heart is not in it. Whatever you do from your heart is powerful. The Bible says the earnest, heartfelt prayer of a righteous man or woman avails much (see James 5:16). I can tell when my prayers are not heartfelt. I can tell when they are real and when my desires and motives are in alignment with God. My life is powerful when I am fully committed to Him. Life takes on new meaning and new purpose. A new power begins to flow through me.

Are you hungry for a life of power? I am tired of duty. I am tired of obligation. I am tired of religion. It is mechanical, ritualistic, dead and dry. All the other faiths in the world can be dry and religious, but Christianity is meant to be a life-giving relationship. It is meant to be spilling out of us because our hearts are full of Jesus. And that same Spirit that raised Jesus from the dead dwells in us and quickens life to our bodies (see Romans 8:10–11).

God can give you a new heart. He can give you new dreams, new desires and new goals. But it is your job to guard your heart and not let the enemy steal your first love. Call it the enemy, call it life, call it other people—whatever it is, do not let it steal your first love.

"And because iniquity shall abound, the love of many shall wax cold" (Matthew 24:12 KJV). I wonder, are you waxing cold today, disconnecting, backsliding? Can you not feel the anointing anymore? If so, your heart has become distant. When you cannot feel Jesus the way you used to, you might think something is wrong with your church or your family. It is not. It is you.

The Holy Spirit knows the condition of your heart. He has something more for you because He loves you. Do not live below the standard of a child of God. We are supposed to be the most blessed, most powerful, most loving, most serving, most unified and most forgiving people on the face of the earth!

If you recognize that you have already grown lukewarm, that is okay. Admit it openly to God. Ask Him to give you back your first love. If you will ask and keep on asking, He will give it back. And when you have it again, guard it like never before. Hard situations will come, but if you draw a line in the sand, you will never again lose it. You will never give your love to something or someone of lesser value than God.

The Wounded Heart

The wounded heart is a heart that is infected by hurt. It is a bleeding heart. It is focused on self and is resistant to God's rule. Demons are attracted to wounded hearts as sharks are to blood in the water. The most dangerous animals in the world are wounded animals. The most dangerous people in the world are wounded people. Hurting people hurt people. How many times have you heard that said?

The wounded heart is full of unforgiveness, resentment and bitterness. Are you still talking about something that happened twenty years ago? Are you keeping an injustice alive that you have not been able to forgive? You have been deeply offended. True, what they did to you was wrong. You have a right to be hurt and offended. But you do not have a right to foster unforgiveness. Remember that even the jail warden spends his life in jail. He is just on the other side of the criminal's bars. Do you really want to imprison yourself with the one or ones who hurt you?

Maybe you do not want to forgive. You are feeding your pain. You are rehearsing the sin against you. Your mind is going crazy with trust issues, bitter thoughts, hatred and ideas for revenge. Listen, you are in this world around sinful, hurting people. And you yourself are guilty of hurting other people at one point or another. A wounded heart left untreated can develop infection and bleeding. The only means of prevention is to do as the Bible tells us and bring every thought into captivity to the obedience of Christ (see 2 Corinthians 10:5). How do we do that? I am going to teach you right now.

Babysit your thoughts. Like kids, they are active every second. They are busy! Don't believe me? How many thoughts have gone through your mind since you sat down to read this book? We have hundreds and thousands of thoughts over the course of a day. Babysit them. Think about what you are thinking about. Arrest the thoughts you find are contrary to the Word of God and to what God would want you to think about. You know what you should be thinking. Pure. Just. Noble. "Think about things that are excellent and worthy of praise" (Philippians 4:8).

If today you say, "My heart is wounded," I want you to feel relief. Recognizing is the first step toward healing your heart. As we discussed, most wounded hearts are the byproduct of unforgiveness. Someone wronged you. Someone hurt you. They lied to you. They betrayed you. You thought they were one way, but they broke your trust. Unforgiveness left unchecked will become bitterness. Bitterness poisons, and this is the sin that causes hearts to be wounded.

But the good news is that forgiveness is your antidote. God says to forgive those who wrong you. That does not mean what they did to you was okay or that it is water under the bridge. It means that you will no longer police justice being served. You will release it to God and allow Him to deal with the wrong as He sees fit. In doing this, you free yourself to move forward, to live again and to be healthy in your spirit, soul, mind and emotions.

"Even if what they did to me hurts so deep?"

Yes. What they did was wrong, but we still have to forgive. It is a spiritual principle: Jesus spilled His perfect blood for every sin we would ever commit before we were born. He says, "If I so freely forgive you, I require you to forgive others."

Because we live in this broken world, we will experience hurt and offense. I am glad forgiveness is choice and not a feeling. You might not feel like forgiving, but you can still choose to do so. In fact, as a believer who has been commanded to forgive, it is very good that you do not have to wait to be inspired to forgive based on your feelings. You can forgive simply because it is God's way of doing things.

Forgiveness frees you, and God wants you free. You will feel light. You will feel so good when you forgive. You will feel God's love. The Bible tells us to not receive the grace of God in vain (see 2 Corinthians 6:1). God's grace is sufficient, which means enough. It is strong enough to help you forgive. It is power available to you when someone betrays you, when someone abuses you or when someone hurts you.

God wants to bring healing to your life today, but you have to lay down your pride, your offenses, your complacency or your bitterness. You must surrender and say, "I need a heart revival." You are going to have to decide to forgive.

The Hardened Heart

Have you begun to be religious? Are you putting other things before God? The Bible says that David was a man after God's own heart, and yet David killed a man. He was an adulterer. He certainly did not do everything right. He made a couple of critically bad decisions. But David was quick to repent. Being quick to repent means everything to God. David sinned, but he had a soft heart—not a hardened heart—before God.

When we are quick to repent for backsliding and being lukewarm, for being religious or for holding on to unforgiveness, it does not take us a month or a year to repent. Those are signs that our heart is still soft. But if we do not repent quickly or do not want to repent at all, sin begins to establish itself in our life.

A hardened heart is a disobedient heart. It is a wounded heart that bled out and drew the enemy in. It is a heart that rejects God's all-sufficiency. It rejects the strength that is made perfect in our weakness. You can forgive when you have Jesus in your heart. Without Him, your countenance changes for the worse. I have seen it happen repeatedly.

Let's forgive quickly so that unforgiveness does not become a root of bitterness within us. Let's forgive quickly so that our hearts do not harden and encrust with a mistrust for God and others. You will have more blessing when you forgive. Obedience brings blessing.

The Broken Heart

The broken heart is one that does not resist God. God can train and tame a heart like this. It is fully surrendered. It is humble and yielded. A broken heart is one that says, "God, do whatever You want with my life. I am tired of being in charge of it. I give up my rights. I submit to You."

The Bible says to submit to God first, then resist the devil and he will flee (see James 4:7). If you are resisting the devil and he is not fleeing, check your heart to see if it is yielded. I just gave you a revelation right there. Yield your rights. God is close to those who are submitted and surrendered.

Brokenness is the way that God deals with our independence. It is the way He deals with our rebellion. It is the way He deals with our self-sufficiency, our pride, our complacency and our sin. He says, "I cannot take you higher or deeper if there is a rebellion inside you. I have to break your heart."

You have a great purpose, but you cannot reach it until you are fully surrendered. You might say, "I'm happy where I am." But no! We have to be changing constantly. We cannot be at the spiritual level we were last month or last week or we will become complacent. We cannot! That is us conforming and falling into religion. And if you are not changing from glory to glory, you are not moving forward with God. You are not standing still. You are going backward! There is no such thing as standing still.

After you get saved, God takes you through a process of sanctification. Sanctification is a sovereign act of God. He sets you apart so that His purposes can be accomplished. This is how God transforms us into His image and likeness. This is how He breaks our stubborn rebellion. When you have a

73

broken heart, you offer worship, you respond in prayer and you serve God and others.

God looks at a broken heart as a sacrifice. And what falls on sacrifices? Fire. God is looking for a broken heart so that He can put His fire and His power in it. I can teach, preach, pray or prophesy. I can experience the best worship and sit under the greatest anointing during which the atmosphere can be charged with the glory of God, but if my heart is wrong, I will not be able to retain what God is speaking to me.

"The sacrifice you desire is a broken spirit. You will not reject a broken and repentant heart, O God" (Psalm 51:17). A heart that is broken with godly sorrow over sin, one that is humble and thoroughly repentant, God will not despise. We need broken hearts.

God has so much He wants to give you. He wants to make you a leader, but He cannot do it with all these obstacles in your life. God cannot take you to the Promised Land with all this mess in the way. He needs you broken; He needs you yielded. You need to get tired of running your own life. Surrender your heart, finances, love life, spouse and half-hearted, powerless Christianity. Say this with me: *I am tired of complacency. I am tired! Lord, break me. Break my heart. Make my heart sensitive to what is on Your heart. I need a heart revival.*

5 | What Revival Will Cost You

Can I shoot straight with you? Revival is going to cost you something. Anything that is worth anything is going to cost something. Discipleship demands sacrifice. Pursuing God will come with personal costs. You will have to deny yourself. You will suffer persecution. Friends and family may turn their backs on you. You may get passed over for that promotion at work. But I am here to tell you that it is going to be worth it all. Being a disciple for Christ is going to cost you, but the price you will pay is still an incredible bargain. If it costs you everything, it is still a bargain!

"I plead with you to give your bodies to God because of all he has done for you. Let them be a living and holy sacrifice —the kind he will find acceptable. This is truly the way to worship him" (Romans 12:1). Do you live a holy life? Are you evaluating where you may not be modeling holiness? Are you living with someone but not married? You say, "But we're in love." That is the world's way; that is not God's way. As followers of Christ, we are to live holy lives that are acceptable to God. That is called reasonable service.

All In and On Fire

I told you before that God would rather you be cold than lukewarm. We read this in Revelation 3:15–16. God says that He will spit you out of His mouth if you are lukewarm. Hard words.

God sent His Son, Jesus, to die a cruel death in which He was tortured by mankind so that you and I could be saved. The way I see it is, if my God did that, the least that I can give back to Him is my "reasonable service." That is to give Him all of me. I cannot be lukewarm, and you cannot either. Not in this hour. We have to be all in and on fire. That is the only way we are going to experience a personal revival and see a revival sweep our nation and the world.

How do you get to this place of being all in and on fire for God? How do you get to the place where your priorities are aligned with God, and He is at the top of your list?

Troubles come. Life happens. It is hard to get passionate about anything, let alone stay passionate, when curve balls are flying at you. To be all in and on fire for God, you need to be aware of your enemy's tactics. Do you think he wants you in right relationship with God? Do you think he wants you to experience revival? No! He has come to steal, kill and destroy. That is why you have to be aware of his tricks, the smoke and mirrors he uses to deter you from the path that is getting you somewhere.

Know Your Enemy's Tactics

A quick snapshot of how the enemy works in your life is the parable of the sower (see Matthew 13). This is how he keeps you from experiencing revival and growing in your faith. When you do not hear the Word of God, or you hear it but do not understand it, you should know something is wrong. It is a symptom of a condition of the heart.

In the natural, we usually know when someone is having a heart attack because they talk about having chest pain. They say that they feel weak or light-headed. They talk about pain in their arm or shoulder. They have shortness of breath. They might be exhausted for no reason or even vomit. It is good that we know these symptoms because recognizing them early enough can save a life. Likewise, we need to know the symptoms of the conditions of the heart that we discussed in the previous chapter. We must be vigilant to check ourselves from time to time.

In the parable of the sower, our hearts are represented by the soil. We can learn from this passage how the enemy operates so that we can protect ourselves from his tactics. We can keep our soil healthy and receptive to the Word of God. We can make sure God's Word can root itself deeply in our hearts.

In the parable of the sower, we read that a farmer goes out to his field. The field represents the heart. The farmer goes into that field to sow seeds. The wicked one comes and snatches away what was sown by the farmer in a variety of ways. One seed falls on the rocks (a hardened heart) and is stolen by the birds. One seed falls on shallow, stony ground (a wounded heart). This seed develops a shallow root system and then wilts under the hot sun. One seed falls among the thorns (a lukewarm heart), which represents the cares of this life, and it is choked out. But one seed falls on the fertile soil (a healthy heart), and it produces a bountiful harvest.

What is the condition of your heart? When tribulation or persecution arise because of your walk with God, will you lose your faith in the Word? Are you the kind of believer who tries to grow in God but when you encounter challenges you immediately stumble? Do you feel choked out by the cares of this world and the deceitfulness of riches? It is okay to admit it, if that is how your heart has been, because you do not have to stay that way. You can make the choice to be fertile soil.

A believer who cultivates fertile soil hears the Word, loves the Word and gets excited about the things of God. But more than that, they spend personal time in the Word. They feast on it. They chew on it. They digest it. They meditate on it. They push in deeper, and that takes their roots deeper. They develop a root system that will nourish them when hard times come—and they will come. They stay free of the things of this world that entrap and entangle so that they will not be choked out.

I want you to have spiritual ears and understanding. I want you to have a sensitive, soft-soil heart. I want you to produce a hundredfold harvest. You must watch out for sin, complacency, unforgiveness and offense. These are stones and weeds that can work their way into your heart soil. They separate you from God and cause the enemy to be able steal the Word from you.

Disobedience Leads to Silence

Disobedience takes many forms. One form is outright rebellion against God. He told you to do one thing, and like Jonah from the story about Jonah and the whale in the Bible, you are traveling in the opposite direction. Do not worry—there is a fish belly waiting for you. You will have plenty of time to reconsider your decision while you are there.

Oftentimes, that is what God allows. He allows a crisis, like being swallowed by a huge fish at sea, to become your breaking point. If you are walking in disobedience, you need to be broken for your own good.

Some people blame God. They are mad at Him because things did not turn out the way they expected. They thought He meant one thing when He meant another, and in their anger, they forgot what He has already done for them. They put up a wall. They say, "I don't want anything to do with God anymore." They push Him away. Let me just say that God is a gentleman. He might come back a second time, giving you a second chance at obedience. Then again, if you push Him away, He may just leave you alone.

Every time you disobey the voice of the Lord, His voice will get a little bit softer and a little harder to hear. Eventually you will not be able to hear it. So if you want to miss out on all that God has for you, just accommodate your disobedience. Desensitize your ears to the voice of the Lord. Just know that if you do, you are going to want Him to come back one day.

> EVERY TIME YOU DISOBEY THE VOICE OF THE LORD, HIS VOICE WILL GET A LITTLE BIT SOFTER AND A LITTLE HARDER TO HEAR.

If you have been walking in disobedience, I encourage you to repent and return to the place where you last heard His voice. Get realigned with God. Get rid of that foolish friend. Get rid of that unsaved boyfriend or girlfriend. Stop going to the places you know you should not go. Surrender your heart. Break yourself, or sin will break you.

Circumcise Your Heart

Jesus quoted a prophecy made by Isaiah about the condition of the people's hearts. He said:

> "When you hear what I say,
> you will not understand.
> When you see what I do,
> you will not comprehend.
> For the hearts of these people are hardened,
> and their ears cannot hear,
> and they have closed their eyes—
> so their eyes cannot see,
> and their ears cannot hear,
> and their hearts cannot understand,
> and they cannot turn to me
> and let me heal them."
>
> Matthew 13:14–15

It is a sad thing that so many people who call themselves Christians have hardened hearts. They cannot see or hear spiritually anymore. Their hearts cannot understand. As a result, God cannot have His perfect will for their lives. He wants relationship with them. He wants to heal them. He wants to revive them. But the condition of their hearts prevents Him from manifesting His perfect will in their lives. Will He have His way in your life?

Today, if you let God, He will circumcise your heart. He will remove the hardness that has encrusted itself around the very thing He desires most. He will remove the problems, the hurts, the offenses, the rejection, the addictions, the sin and the rebellion that has gotten in the way of your relationship with Him. He will remove your spiritual dryness, your apathy and lukewarmness. This condition of your heart truly is at the root of all your problems.

You cannot have a personal revival with a bad heart condition. You must have a heart that is soft and pure. You must have a heart that is able to receive all that God wants to give you. This is why He is after your heart. If God has your heart, He will know—and you will know—that you are all in!

Do You Really Want It?

Do you want a move of God? Do you really want it? Do you want the fire, the glory, the next level in your walk of faith? Do you want the supernatural, the deliverance and the demonstrations? I want it all. I think you do, too.

I am not satisfied to stay where I am. I want the glory to come so that our cities hear the sound of the Lord as we worship together on Sunday mornings. I want to see them coming off the street into the church to get right with God. We have to save our cities. I declare that our cities will be saved. I declare that gangs will be saved and delivered. I declare that God is raising up more deliverers. I declare that we are going to push back the principalities, powers and rulers of darkness over these cities so far that they are going to forget where they were even assigned!

Every time you hesitate to go all in with God, it shows. Hesitate to obey and it shows God where your heart is. If He says, "I want you to be an intercessor," and you say, "No, I don't have time," that is rebellion. If He says, "I want you to go here," then go. Do not hesitate. Do not rebel. Do not be stubborn. You need to surrender.

God has more for you and your family than what you are experiencing today. Think of the legacy you will leave when you get this message inside of you. A healthy heart is supremely important to God. That means it has been broken and has healed. It is pure and pliable. It is ready to receive the Word of the Lord and respond to it by yielding a harvest.

Remember, your trust is not in man. Your trust is not in your gifts. Your trust is in God. That is why you do not resist the change He brings. You say yes to God, and if God says to go right, you go right. If He says, "Don't marry that person," you don't. A healthy heart is what God is looking for. When your heart is healthy, you will begin to experience a personal revival.

6 | How to Have a Rain Revival

I t is a sad thing that Christians rarely use the word *revival* anymore. Maybe it is because many of them do not really care about revival. They think they can live without it just fine. The problem is that we will not be victorious in this life without the Spirit of God, without a touch of the supernatural. For this reason, I want to show you how you can have a personal revival.

There is a revival that needs to take place in you, because revival does not happen outside until it happens inside. Something has got to happen inside you so that it can ultimately happen in our cities and nation. In the book of Deuteronomy, we read the words of Joshua to the people of Israel (see 11:13–17). In this passage, Joshua was drawing a line in the sand and telling them they had to make a choice. It was going to be either this way or that way, but they could no longer occupy a gray space. He said:

"If you carefully obey the commands I am giving you today, and if you love the LORD your God and serve him with all your heart and soul, then he will send the rains in their proper seasons—the early and late rains—so you can bring in your harvests of grain, new wine, and olive oil."

Deuteronomy 11:13–14

When we see statements like this in the Bible, we need to understand they are conditional. Really, everything in the Bible is conditional for you to receive something. If you will do this thing, then this other thing will happen. No one knows if you are going to do it or not, because you have free will. Even God will not stop you from doing what you want to do. That is why Joshua prefaces his statement by saying, "It is up to you. You make the choice."

In this passage, Joshua lays out exactly what must happen for you to receive the seasonal rains from God and the harvest of your actions:

1. You have to obey.
2. You have to love.
3. You have to serve.

In the Bible, rain signifies the harvest. If there is rain, a harvest is sure to follow. It makes sense when you consider that Israel was kind of an agrarian society. They needed the rain for their livestock and their fields. Deuteronomy 11:14 promised the Israelites harvests from the fields and lush pastureland for their livestock and families. "He will give you lush pastureland for your livestock, and you yourselves will have all you want to eat" (verse 15). These are the benefits every farmer would want, right? But God's conditional promise came with a warning.

> "But be careful. Don't let your heart be deceived so that you turn away from the LORD and serve and worship other gods. If you do, the LORD's anger will burn against you. He will shut up the sky and hold back the rain, and the ground will fail to produce its harvests. Then you will quickly die in that good land the LORD is giving you."
>
> Deuteronomy 11:16–17

Ouch! That is a severe consequence, don't you think? God is saying to us through Joshua, "Why would I send the rain to you and why would I give you a harvest when you have not been obedient? When you have not loved? When you have not served?"

Too many believers want something to happen for them, but they have not done anything to warrant it. They have not been obedient with their gifts and talents. They have not planted anything. They have not shown love or been a help to their friends or neighbors. Why should God send rain when you have not done your part? Why, if you have not tilled or dug or worked the land, if you have not taken seed and planted it in the ground, should God rain upon you? There is nothing to grow.

We must own our decisions. We have to be able to say, "I am the only one who can decide if my future holds blessings or curses. I can't blame my boss. I can't blame my family. I can't blame anybody for how I live. I can only blame myself." Instead, many people complain that God has blessed someone else more—as if that motivates God to bestow blessings. Listen, God does not bless you because you point out someone who is doing better than you. He blesses what you do that is in line with His will.

Be Careful

As we read Deuteronomy 11, we see that God is waiting to bless us with the rain, both the early and the late rain, in its proper season. What does that tell us? It tells us that we do not need rain all the time. When it makes sense in terms of growing your harvest, He will deliver the rain you need. He will also deliver the sunlight. He will deliver whatever you need in its proper season.

God gives you the harvest. Your boss does not give it to you. Neighbors do not give it to you. Your deceased, rich aunt in Los Angeles does not give it to you. God gives it to you. In acknowledgment of this, you give to God, and God gives back to you everything you need for a harvest.

The warning to be careful was given because Israel had a tendency to turn away from God. Many times throughout their history, they were found worshiping false gods. We also see at those times that their harvest withered, and they often experienced negative consequences. Joshua was calling them to stop the cycle, to be aware of their fleshly tendencies and to be committed to their decision to follow God. Only then would they receive their harvest. "He will shut up the sky and hold back the rain, and the ground will fail to produce its harvests" (Deuteronomy 11:17).

I do not know about you, but I would not want the Lord's anger to burn like that against me. Who would have thought that sometimes the devil has nothing to do with the problems you are facing? Maybe your problem is that God shut up the rain, God stopped your blessing and now you have no harvest. Why? Because you have not done what He commanded you to do.

Not only will the Lord's anger burn against you, but you will quickly die in the good land the Lord has for you (see verse 17). Wow. God gave Israel a choice, and He is giving us the same choice today. It is a choice that leads to blessings or curses.

The only way the devil can do something to you is if God steps out of the way and lets him make his move. If God is with you, the devil can do nothing. But you do not want God in your life. You do not want Him calling the shots. You like being in control. Don't worry. He will walk away. He will not stay where He is not wanted. Just realize you are leaving yourself susceptible to the enemy's takedown when you call the shots for your life.

I do not think you are that person. I think you are like me. We want the rain. We want the harvest. We want revival to take place in our lives. We are opening our hearts wide and asking God to do something great in us.

Today is a day of change. May it be a life-changing day, a character-changing day. May we leave the old flesh aside and unstrap the weights that drag us back and slow us down. We want to run this race and finish it. God, help us to see a revival take place in our lives, our homes and our communities!

The Earnest Prayer of Elijah

Look with me at James 5:16. "Confess your sins to each other and pray for each other so that you may be healed. The earnest prayer of a righteous person has great power and produces wonderful results."

An earnest prayer is a sincere prayer, something heartfelt. An unrighteous person is not going to offer an earnest prayer because he is only praying to receive. He is in crisis mode. But when the crisis is over, so is the praying. The rest of his life, he just leaves God alone. But when a righteous person prays, you do not have to worry about the answer. You are guaranteed a good result.

James goes on to tell us that the prophet Elijah was just as human as we are, but the result of his earnest prayer was that no rain fell in Israel for three and a half years. Then, when he changed his prayer, the rain fell, and the crops began to grow again. I want you to get this: If Elijah could be like us in our passions, we can be like him in our prayers.

You might say, "Oh, but Elijah was a mighty prophet of God. I am certainly not. He witnessed unbelievable miracles and called fire down from heaven. I can't do that!" You are right. Elijah was wrapped in a mantle of supernatural power and experience. I know he appears unapproachable. You and I would never say we could be like Elijah. He is too dynamic of a character. But James says that we can. We can pray and spend time with God just like Elijah did. We can see God do miraculous things through us as well.

James knew a lot about prayer. His book says more about the doctrine of prayer than any other book in the New Testament. Prayer was his life's discipline. He was not a theorist; he was a practitioner who earned the nickname "camel knees" for the callouses on his knees that came from his time in prayer.[1]

For this reason, I think we need to strongly consider what he is saying. If we can discover some of the characteristics of Elijah's life, maybe we can follow his pattern and get a similar result.

When you study Elijah, you learn quickly that there is no historical record about his origin. We do not know much more about him than where he came from, but James said he had problems just like us. He had life-challenges like us. He had people who did not like him. He was lonely and fearful at times. He even doubted God.

Despite his humanity, Elijah became a mighty prophet of God. He was a miracle worker. He was a prayer warrior. He really prayed. His prayers were pure and deeply sincere. He was not trivial. He was not petty. His prayers were not, "O Lord, bless the food in Jesus' name." His seriousness and faith and determination meant something when he prayed. Clearly, if we want to model Elijah and see greater results in our lives, we must learn to pray with earnestness and determination. That is what makes the difference. If Elijah could be similar to you in his passions, then you can be similar to him in your prayer life.

The story of Elijah that James was referring to is found in 1 Kings 17 and 18. Here is the backstory: King Ahab and his wife, Jezebel, were bad rulers. Part of the reason they were bad was they put four hundred prophets of Baal on their staff. We see quickly that as far as Ahab was concerned, Elijah was a troublemaker. He was such a problem that Ahab released hitmen to find him. But no matter where the king or his hitmen looked, they could not find Elijah. One day, Elijah told his servant, "Go tell the king I'm coming to see him. No need to find me; I'll find him." He approached the very ones who wanted to kill him. He said to King Ahab, "As surely as the LORD, the God of Israel, lives . . . there will be no dew or rain during the next few years until I give the word!" (1 Kings 17:1). How about that, king?

Three and a half years pass without a drop of rain having fallen on the land. Everyone is suffering. At that point, Elijah came to King Ahab again and said to him, "Go get something to eat and drink, for I hear a mighty rainstorm coming!" (1 Kings 18:41). He sent the king away, he approached the altar at the time of the evening sacrifice and then he prayed.

Have you ever thought about how much prayer is involved in your harvest? If you want a harvest, you had better get praying. Little prayer, little harvest. No prayer, no harvest. Much prayer, much harvest.

It is that simple.

Elijah walked up to the altar and prayed. He prayed before the miracle happened. He could not hear the rain with his physical ears, but he heard it with his ears of faith. He prayed, "God of Abraham, Isaac, and Jacob, prove today that you are God in Israel and that I am your servant. Prove that I have done all this at your command" (1 Kings 18:36). The drought had gone on for years. Everything was dry. Everything was dead. They needed the rain to bring life again.

If rain means you get a harvest, drought means you need to repent. I am speaking to you. If you are in a drought right now, something needs to change in your spiritual life. Drought is an indicator to which you must pay attention. It might be that God wants you to repent of some sin you have been harboring. Maybe pride is in the way. Maybe your flesh wants to rule. I hope you hear me on this—whatever it is, it is not worth it. If you do not get right with God, you are going to keep facing an inconvenient drought. And drought leads to death. You cannot ignore the drought. You need the rain, the renewal of God, to live.

I can hear people asking, "If God promises that it is going to rain, why do we have to pray about it? The Bible is full of promises. Why do we have to pray for them?" Prayer is the hand of faith that translates your promise into performance. Not only does God ordain the end to what takes place, but He ordains the means. You do not get to choose the way you receive a miracle of God. You have to allow Him to do it His way.

Prayer is not coming to a reluctant God in an attempt to persuade Him to do what He really does not want to do. It is a matter of coming to God with an awareness that we are dependent individuals. We are dependent upon Him. Prayer is the realization that our need is not partial, but total. We do not come to God because we have a little need. We come to God because we totally, not partially, need Him. This is why I repeat to myself frequently, *When I try, I fail. When I trust, I succeed.*

We need change in our lives. We need miracles that only come through fervent prayer. It might be for our family, for our kids, for our parents or for our jobs. But we need something to break. I want to help you break whatever it is that is standing in your way. Even if your family is a mess right now, God is going to work it out. I hear the sound of restoration. Your kids may be away from God, but I see your kids at the altar with their hands lifted high asking God to save them. You may need healing. Your doctors have given up on you. They say they cannot help you anymore. But I see God touching your body and doing a miracle in your life. You have got to see it, too!

My daughter has been sick for 25 years, but our whole family still sees her healed. How long do we wait to see it happen? As long as we have to. Do not give up. Do not give up! You have got to provoke the rain for your revival to come.

If you have had no real experience with our supernatural God, you will have no passion for the things of God. You will have no passionate prayers. And as a result, you will have no rain. If you have been tilling your land and planting seeds, then you are ready for the rain. You have been doing what you can. But you need water, and only God can supply that. I want you to know the rain is coming. When the rain comes, you will be overjoyed.

Elijah had confidence that the rain was coming. He saw the rain before it fell. I saw my church full before it was ever full. It is full now. The balconies are full. It is not really big enough to put all of our people in one service, which, praise God, we did not have that "problem" before. In the middle of the worst time that we have had as a church, back in 2009 to 2010 during the recession, God told us to build a new building so that we could make space for children's church. I saw kids in my spirit, and I said, "We need to have this thing!" I saw it before it was built. I saw the football field we now have before it was made. I saw a fitness center before it was established. This is how faith works!

How did Elijah know the rain was coming? Because he communicated regularly with God. Let me just say, I think we overcomplicate communication with God. When we have been saved for a while, we develop the thought that there is a certain way you have got to pray, as if you have to be really good at prayer to receive from God. But prayer is nothing more than talking with your heavenly Father.

"Well, I don't know if I could talk to God." Show me your phone. How many people do you talk to every day? And how many minutes do you go on in senseless conversations that go nowhere?

I love new converts. They pray like, "Hi, God. My name is Robert. Last Wednesday, I don't know what happened, but I went to an altar, and I asked You to come into my life.

And wow, since then, I still can't believe what has happened to me! I'm pretty much on fire here, and I don't know what to tell You. But I just want to tell You I love You and thanks. I'll talk to You later."

I got saved when I was a college football player. So did a guy I knew. He was told to pray whatever was in his heart, so he began, "Lord, give me that funky feeling!" That was his salvation prayer! And guess what. God gave it to him. I asked him, "How do you feel?" And he said, "I just want to run up those stairs to heaven right now!" He still has that funky feeling today.

You cannot cause the rains of refreshing to fall in your life all by yourself. You are just flesh. You cannot take on the things of the world. You need your supernatural Father to help you, to go and do for you. When I realized this, my prayer life changed. When I trusted God, I began to succeed. I stopped failing so much. I grew in confidence that I could trust Him with everything. Now I trust Him with my finances. I trust Him with my kids. I know that I am not able to raise my kids correctly and teach them everything they need to know to succeed in life, but I trust God to help me.

We've got to learn to weave prayer into the fabric of our lives. There are three characteristics of Elijah's prayer that released the rain upon Israel that I will share with you in the next chapter. I believe we can employ those same characteristics in our prayer time to end the drought in our personal lives and provoke the rain to fall. Those three characteristics are that he prayed with determination, he expected a miracle and he celebrated the results.

7 | Three Characteristics of an Effective Prayer Life

In the last chapter, I began to talk to you about how to have a rain revival. I showed you in the book of James where he spoke about how the great prophet Elijah provoked the rain to fall from heaven. James said that Elijah was a man just like us. He experienced pain, he had fears and he suffered from things like anxiety and depression. He went through many difficult moments in his life. But Elijah was a tremendous, mighty man of God, and part of what made him so powerful was his effective prayer life.

Elijah ended a drought in Israel that lasted for several years, and he provoked the rain to fall by doing three things in his prayer life: He prayed with determination, he expected a miracle and he celebrated the results. Let's take a closer look at each of these characteristics of his prayer life and how we can incorporate them into our own.

Elijah Prayed with Determination

Determination is earnestness. An earnest prayer is spoken in deep sincerity; it is not trivial or petty. While there was still no cloud in the sky, Elijah said to the king, "Listen, go get something to eat and drink, because you do not really care about this spiritual stuff. Why don't you just go?" Doubters need to go when you are praying with determination. They do not want to see you blessed. They are jealous. They are non-supportive. You need to get away from them so that God can bless you. Turn off your phone. Say goodbye to a few "friends." Get with people who actually support you, believe in you and hope that you will be successful. You need their encouragement, not the garbage of negativity.

I am sure Ahab looked up when he went out to eat that day. I am sure he looked around and thought, *There is not a cloud in the sky! It has been sunny for three and a half years. Elijah has lost his mind.* But Elijah was in close, constant communication with God. When he knelt on his knees, God began to show him things. He heard the rain. He heard the harvest coming.

"How can you see something when your head is down, Elijah?"

"God shows me with the eyes of faith. He lets me hear with the ears of faith. I don't need to see it. I can see it in the spirit. You can, too, if you spend time with God."

You may not be healed today, but I see something through the eyes of faith. I see that it is finished. How can it be finished when you are still on medicine or when you are crippled and can barely walk? Because I see through the eyes of faith what is coming. Because I pray and spend time with God.

When I came to Modesto, California, years ago, I saw our church in the natural. It was running one service a week, and that service was only filled to the eighth row back. I cried and asked God, "Why did You even send us to Modesto? What is in Modesto? There is nothing here!"

But when He gave me eyes of faith, I saw the church full. I saw it so full that we could not get all the people in, and we had to have multiple service times. Today, we have five different services and multiple campuses. When you spend time with God, there is always something to see in the spirit before it manifests.

There is something not yet visible that God will show you when you spend time with Him. You can see and feel the invisible. Your marriage may be at the bottom of the ocean, but you can hear with your ears that resurrection is coming. Restoration is coming. Your son or daughter may be away from God and involved in all kinds of worldly things, but you can hear God say that He is getting ready to put a rope around them and draw them back.

You have to get on your knees to hear in the spirit. You have to provoke the rain for your revival to come. *You provoke the rain* when your victory is not complete. *You provoke the rain* when your enemies have gathered against you and when unbelievers ask you, "Where is your God?" *You provoke the rain* when people are waiting for you to fail, when your family is in generational bondage, when your debt is mounting and your income is low. When your destiny has been embalmed and buried, when the tears have become a regular affair, when you could not smile if you needed to— that is when you are in the best position to provoke the rain. Praise the Lord!

The devil has messed with you long enough, has he not? It is time to get your stride back, get your fire back and get the rain that will bring the harvest back into your life.

If you have no real experience with our supernatural God, you will have no passion for God. You will not care about prayer. Some people feel the rain while others just get wet. Those in need of a harvest pray for the rain. Those who do not pray for a harvest get tired of the rain. Rain becomes bothersome. It is not something they want. It messes up the car they just washed yesterday. It is a hassle, an inconvenience.

If you are going to have your own personal revival, it is going to be up to you. Nobody can pray it down for you. You need to grow up and take responsibility for your prayer life—for your life in general.

> **SOME PEOPLE WANT THE BENEFITS OF PRAYER WITHOUT PRAYING, AND IT IS NOT GOING TO HAPPEN.**

I need some rain in my life. How about you? How about some rain of prosperity? How about another job? How about a healed marriage? How about a healed body? I need to have a deeper relationship with the Lord. I cannot live another day in drought conditions. I cannot live in a dry land any longer. I will do what it takes to have revival. Will you?

Some people want the benefits of prayer without praying, and it is not going to happen. I want you to pray with me right now.

God, I need You to wash my mind, to wash away my sin, to change my life and to remove the weights that have attached themselves to me. I want to be free to the point that I can dream again, Lord. There is something better. There is abundant life. I have not lived it yet, and it is my fault. I need to change. I need to change my thinking, to change what I believe and to change my habits. I must discern the difference between what is important and what is not important. My flesh cannot run my life or control my mind anymore. It is time for me to have life. I ask You now to rain on me. Bring me a harvest in areas that I need and areas I do not even know exist. You know. Show me how real You are. But first, let me show You how committed I am. I am all in. From this day forward, I am all in with You. In Jesus' name, Amen.

Elijah Expected a Miracle

After Elijah sent King Ahab out to eat and drink, he climbed to the top of the Mount Carmel (see 1 Kings 18:42). He bowed low to the ground and began to pray with his face between his knees. He prayed with determination. He prayed with expectation. And he saw the future when he was on his knees.

Elijah told his servant, "Go. Look toward the sea."

The servant returned and said, "I went, but I didn't see anything" (see verse 43).

Did that shake Elijah? Not at all. He told his servant to go look again six more times. Time after time, the servant announced there was not even a cloud in the sky. It was the sunniest it could be. There was no sign of rain. The servant must have thought there was something wrong with Elijah.

How many times would you have made that trip? How many times, if God kept telling you, would you have kept praying? Kept knocking? Kept asking? Kept going back to look for rain? Would you have thought, *There is nothing there. It is not working. Why keep believing? Why keep praying?*

Elijah was determined enough and expectant enough to tell his servant to make however many trips that were necessary. He said in essence, "I'm not going to give up until I see this miracle take place." How about you? Will you keep going until you see your family restored? Until you see your kids saved? Until your healing manifests? It does not matter how long it takes. I am telling you, just keep going!

We are bunch of babies today. We go here and there whining that we do not see anything; however, the battle is not over. We are still in the war. You might be behind right now, but I read the end of the story and it says we win. We win in the end. You have to realize we are going to win this thing. There is no reason to quit.

Seven times. The servant went to look seven times. Elijah kept asking, "What do you see?" It does not always happen right away. Get rid of your watch. Do not put God on your timetable. Do not tell God when He needs to perform your miracle. He does not have to listen to you. He has got a purpose in everything He does. You need to learn to trust Him and His timing.

On the seventh time, Elijah's servant returned. "Okay, finally, I see a little cloud about the size of a man's hand rising from the sea" (see verse 44). It was a fist-sized cloud, still not a real sign of rain, but Elijah got all excited. He shouted, "Hurry! Tell the king! Tell him to climb into his chariot! He better get back home before the rain comes!"

Shortly after, the sky began to turn black. It was a gradual change, little by little. They had to have patience in waiting for the rain, and so do we. It is not going to happen right away. We will have to wait on it. Soon enough, the dark sky was filled with heavy wind. A wind revival was taking place (we will talk more about the wind revival in our next chapter). It brought a terrific rainstorm.

Do you have expectant faith? Are you looking for something, or have you given up looking? Are you believing and asking God for something, or have you decided it is not going to happen? Maybe you have said, "Why look anymore? Maybe I should just quit looking for my miracle. Maybe I should just quit believing for my child or husband or wife or parent to get saved." But I say no, keep looking. Do not give up. Keep searching and believing. Keep going back. Keep praying. Keep pursuing. Do not give up!

I pray that you keep believing that God wants to do something miraculous in your life. If you expect nothing and give up, guess what? You will not win. If you stop halfway in the race, you should not expect the medal. God does not give out participation awards. He does not have a trophy that says, "I tried." He gives out completion awards at the finish line.

I want you to think about your family. Is there someone in your family that would be hard to believe to be saved? If you got a phone call and they said they just got saved and filled with the Spirit, you would drop the phone and say, "No way! There's no way!" I have some like that. I would be shocked if it was him or her. There is no way that person would accept salvation or accept the Holy Spirit. But if God told me that person was going to get saved, that it was going to rain, I would just receive it even though it was so unbelievable.

God is the God of unbelievable acts, unbelievable miracles. Do not miss God. Go back and look again. Keep looking. Eventually the rain is going to come. And when it does, you need to be looking around. You need to be around positive people who trust and have faith. You need to be around people who will pray with you. You do not need a negative person to tell you it is not going to happen. You need people who will agree with you in faith. You need people who believe that miracles can still come to pass.

Elijah Celebrated the Results

The results of the rain were many. The land was renewed. And Elijah emerged with a new and dynamic authority. This is what happens to you in a rain revival. "Then the LORD gave special strength to Elijah" (1 Kings 18:46).

Is this where you are today? You have kept going. You have kept persevering. You have not given up. You have not quit, sat down or cried about it. You have kept pursuing. When your miracle happens, this supernatural strength is going to fill you. You are going to have a confidence that what you experienced here can be experienced elsewhere in your life. You will not be able to go back after you receive your miracle. You will keep pursuing God for the rest of your life. You will keep going after Him.

So God gave Elijah special strength. He tucked his cloak in his belt, and he ran ahead of Ahab's chariot and horses all the way to the city of Jezreel. Can you believe that? He outran the horses! That is supernatural strength. The power of God came upon him, and the same power will come on you.

It was not Elijah's great prayer language that brought the power. It had nothing to do with the length of his prayer. It had nothing to do with the loudness or the softness of his prayer. It was his determination and expectation to see the Lord perform a miracle.

Get Involved in Your Miracle

It is dangerous to pray because when you pray, you get involved. Maybe the reason you do not have what God wants you to have today is because you are not involved. Why would God give you something when you do not want to be part of the miracle you are believing God will give you?

We read in the New Testament story upon story about Jesus. He was only in ministry for three and a half years. He started at 30 years of age and died at 33, and yet all the books in the world could not contain all of the miracles and all of the things Jesus did within that time (see John 21:25). That does not make sense because we have a lot of information about Jesus in the four gospels; however, what was written was done in the 33 years in His life. That is an eye-opener. We really only know about one month of Jesus' life based upon the documentation. So when we are reading the gospels, we need to ask ourselves what Jesus was doing in that month that was so amazing, so worth noting. What did He do within those days that was so incredible? How did He accomplish so much in such little time? The answer is simple: Jesus would often get up before sunrise and go to a place where He could be alone to pray. He prayed. Faithfully. With determination. With expectation.

If Jesus had to develop the habit of praying daily and hearing from His Father, what should you and I do? How do we get away with skipping this part? How do we look at this discipline of prayer as being something optional?

Prayer is so powerful that Elijah could see the future when he was on his knees. Think about what I just said. Maybe I am not able to look past my nose for what is going on. Maybe my issue is that I keep looking back because I am not on my knees to see my future. Elijah heard the rain while he was on his knees. He heard the miracle on his knees. I am telling you that you can stay where you are, but your position is going to tell us a lot about where your heart is.

If you do not have anything happening on the outside, that means there is not much happening on the inside. You are not above what God wants to do in your life. Maybe you think you can handle everything. If you want to keep God out of your life, that is fine. I will not twist your arm. Just do not ask me why God will not do anything for you when you do not want Him around! God does not owe you anything. You and I owe Him. He already died for us. He already gave His Son for us. He has done it all. You do not need to do it. I do not need to do it. We owe Him, and we cannot pay Him back.

How to Provoke Your Rain Revival

In 2014 the city of Modesto, California, experienced a drought. The city had not had substantial rain for over three years. We did not know when we would have to shut off our water main. We could only use water on certain days. People could only take baths once a week. Everybody started to stink. After three years of drought, our farmers were losing their businesses—losing what they inherited from grandparents. The local economy was failing. We were losing goods and produce.

We invited all the area farmers to the church for a meeting. Many farmers came and stood at the altar. We spoke to them and said, "Okay. Here is the story about Elijah and the rain. We can be like Elijah." And we began to pray. It had been over three years, but that Wednesday it started to pour! The rain came down and saved our land. It saved all the farmers. Believe what you want to believe, but it happened. How crazy is that? But what happened in the Bible happens today, too!

Would you like to know how to provoke the rain to come? Let me give you four keys. Are you ready for them?

Release worry from your life. The beginning of worry is the end of faith. Underline that. If you worry, you remove yourself from faith, and you move into an area of questioning God—every time.

You must have breakthrough faith. Close your eyes and see what is going to happen. Ask God to show you something when your eyes are closed. Ask God to let you hear something. Tell Him you are listening. You need to believe it even when you do not see it. You do not need to talk; you need to hear God say something. It is not what you see. It is what He says.

Pray until something happens. Keep praying for the rain. Who cares if you only saw a cloud? That is not the time to quit! You have got to keep praying. You have got to keep believing. The doctor gave you a good report, but you still have a tumor. Keep praying. Just like the cloud the size of a man's hand, it began small and grew to extra-large. It is a process, but you have to keep praying. So do not give up. Do not stop in the middle of getting your miracle. Do not stop when you see the door cracked open. Bust that door wide open by praying and believing.

Never accept your present position as final. Understand that where you are right now is not your final resting place. Wherever you are financially, it is not where you are going to be. Wherever you are in your marriage, it is not where you are supposed to stay. God has something better than where you are. Amen?

I am going to make this really simple because I have a declaration that I want you to speak out loud. I sense you want to believe God for something: a miracle, a need or provision. You are ready to look for the cloud. So say this with me:

I provoke the heavens to open in the name of Jesus. Every power that has hindered me will be destroyed. My rain of marital, business and financial breakthrough, I provoke you to fall. I call to the Lord God of Elijah and provoke my rain of blessings to fall in the name of Jesus.

If Jesus prayed, you need to pray. You cannot stay the same. Something is going to change in you as you pursue God. Repent of anything that has hindered you from getting your miracles and receiving your blessings. Ask God to take it from you and cleanse you. That is how you provoke the rain and receive your harvest.

I know you need a miracle. You need a breakthrough. I believe you understand now that you cannot stay where you are. You have to change. I pray God leads you to spend time with Him. May revival begin in your life even today!

8 | How to Have a Wind Revival

O nce upon a time, you and I got saved. That was our first revival. The old man passed away and we were made new. We were awakened to know God in a new way. Our relationship moved from impersonal to personal. He became real to us.

We got revived when we got saved, but we need that kind of revival again. One revival is not enough for this lifetime. We need a constant refreshing, a constant deepening of our walk with God and relationship with Him. The psalmist recognized this need when he wrote, "Won't you revive us again, so your people can rejoice in you?" (Psalm 85:6).

Some believers are beaten down. It is not easy to stay joyful in a society that is this negative. We do not have people walking around smiling and joking anymore. We have crowds of people who are upset and sad all the time. I believe this is one of the reasons we do not have widespread revivals anymore. We are content to live without Him. We do not think we need Him. We act as though we are fine without God showing up, fine without talking to Him. We are fine without going to His church, fine without giving. Just fine. It is a lackadaisical, mediocre life at best.

The greatest need in our generation is a heaven-sent revival. You want to get rid of the hate in our nation? The answer is a revival of God. That is the only thing that is going to do it. It is not going to be new laws. It is not going to be a new politician. It is not going to be another topic we need to vote on. It is not going to be enforced by the police. It is going to be that God has intervened in the affairs of men on this earth and brought revival. This is why we must humble ourselves and cry out to Him saying, "Come heal our land!"

You see, when God is glorified, the pursuit of temporary pleasures is abandoned. You will not care about them anymore. Revival will bring great masses of people to their senses. They will wake up to God, many for the very first time.

Did you know that Christians rarely talk about hell anymore? It is not preached from the pulpit in many churches. We talk about faith and goodness and prosperity in heaven, but we do not talk about the reality of hell. When our churches, our communities and our cities experience revival, people will become aware that there is a hell. They will want to get right with God immediately. Hell is a real place.

There are people right now, even Christians, who will not truly glorify God. They offer diluted or polluted worship on Sundays and Wednesdays. They are more concerned with their will than His will, and they have forgotten the price He paid for them and the debt of gratitude they owe.

We were not made for ourselves, friend. We were made for God. Do you understand we are here to worship and honor

God? We are not here for ourselves. Do you realize of what we are made? Dirt. We are made of the same stuff that we vacuum up and throw in the garbage. It does not hold value to us. It is just dirt. We are just dirt. The only thing that is incredible about you and me is the breath that God breathed into us that made us alive. And when His breath is gone, we return back to what we are without Him.

We need a fresh revival. We need a realignment with the truth of who we are and who God is. We need to recommit to follow His better way and surrender our less-than-perfect way of living. It is time we put our personal agendas on the altar.

A Wind Revival

I want you to take a look with me at Ezekiel 37. I strongly encourage you to get out your Bible and read this passage for yourself. This is the prophet Ezekiel's recount of the valley of dry bones. In it, he said that the Lord took hold of him and carried him away by the Spirit to a valley that was filled with bones. A valley filled with bones is not a really happy sight, is it? Basically, it was a landscape of death.

These bones covered the valley floor. It was not just a few; it was an army's worth. They were scattered everywhere, which means these people died at different intervals in their journey. Some of them died at one period of time and some died at another. They may have even died in different years for all we know. Wherever they gave up, that is where their bones came to rest. Each one had his or her own journey, and each one's journey ended uniquely.

Something Ezekiel noticed about these bones that were scattered everywhere is that they were completely dried out.

Why would this be important? Would it not be stating the obvious that these bones were dried out? I think God wanted us to have the picture that these people had not just died—they had been dead so long that their bones had bleached in the sun.

Have you been out in the wilderness? In the Middle East, where Israel is, it can be bleak. It is mostly barren with mountains and terraces. It is a harsh environment. This is where these bones made their final journey. Looking at the surroundings and how bleached and dry the bones were, Ezekiel knew there was no chance for life to return to these people. But God asked Ezekiel, "Son of man, can these bones become living people again?" (Ezekiel 37:3).

How would you have answered God? Would you have said, "Well, I have faith, so yeah." I mean, that would be the right answer even if you did not actually have the faith for it, right? You know that God can do whatever He wants to do. So often we say the right things, but we do not really believe it will happen. This is one reason I like Ezekiel. He was not about fake faith. He answered honestly. "O Sovereign LORD . . . you alone know the answer to that" (verse 3).

The word *sovereign* means that no one can come close to Him. There is no close second. It means only God could say something like, "Come alive," and it would happen. The devil is not eye-to-eye with God. God created him, and God tossed him out of heaven. He does not have the power to bring the dead back to life.

So here is this bleak-as-it-gets wilderness scene with sun-bleached bones lying all over the valley. Really, this is about as sad as it gets. The valley is a picture of death. Ezekiel stood there surveying the facts, and God asked him if something dead could be restored to life. It is important for you to understand that the bones in this passage do not represent people. They represent unresolved things, hopeless situations and failed dreams.[1] In this valley were tens of thousands of these situations and desires that did not end well. The outcomes looked totally dead. There was no way anything good could come out of them.

You may have a marriage that is dead. Your financial situation may be dead. Your child or family member might be on drugs. You do not know what is going to happen to them. You have some hopeless situations in your life. They are bleached, dried-out bones. You believe you are so far away from seeing a resurrection, but this passage is for you today.

"O Sovereign Lord, You alone know the answer," Ezekiel answered. The Lord replied, "Speak a prophetic message to these bones" (verse 4).

Oh, come on! Speak to the bones. And say what?! Say what to the dead thing? I cannot resuscitate this. You cannot resuscitate it. These bones do not have anything left to work with. They are disconnected, dry, not one bit of muscle or skin on them, no organs—just bones. He said, "Say, 'Dry bones, listen to the word of the Lord!'"

Did you know that in the spiritual realm your debt situation can hear you if you speak the Word of the Lord to it? If you do not catch anything else in this chapter, catch this: Your situation that is about as dead as dead can be still has ears if you will speak the Word of the Lord to it.

There Is Power in the Word

We can be so full of complaints when we are looking at unresolved or hopeless situations. But God does not inhabit your complaints. He inhabits your praises. I believe this is what the sovereign Lord says to you today, just as He said it to Ezekiel thousands of years ago. "Look! I am going to put breath [breath is a wind] into you and make you live again" (verse 5).

> **GOD DOES NOT INHABIT YOUR COMPLAINTS. HE INHABITS YOUR PRAISES.**

This describes the creation of Adam. God spoke to the dirt, put His breath in Adam, and Adam was born. All of a sudden, flesh and muscles and skin appeared. And here in Ezekiel, God says to you, "I will put breath into you, and you will come to life. Then you will know that I am the LORD" (verse 6). God will put His breath, His wind and His Spirit into you.

When God breathes on your dry bones, you will come to life again. You will see a miracle. Maybe you do not really know the Lord. You have heard stories about Him and you may even call yourself a Christian, but you have never really gotten right with God. You have never really given Him control of your life. If that is the case, it is time to get serious and get things right with God.

If you need to ask forgiveness, ask. If you need to remove sin, come clean. Remove every hindrance to having a right relationship with Him. If you have strayed, come back to God. Straighten some things out in your life. God forbid you put this book down and turn on the television instead of getting down on your knees and turning your will over to God. If you do, you will lose out in a big way.

Take a moment to pray. Tell the Lord honestly what you are thinking.

Jesus, I need You to take everything. I am tired of half-way. I am tired of being a Christian in name but not in

*action. I am tired of being lazy. I want You to have all
of me. In Jesus' name, Amen.*

Maybe you are discouraged. Maybe it seems to you as if
God has done so much for others but nothing special for you.
You do not feel as if you have your own testimony of His
goodness toward you. You can say, "I know He did it for her,
and I know He did it for him," but you do not know if He
has ever done anything for you. It is time to start speaking
the Word of God to your dead situation over and over again.
Maybe this is the season that your testimony will manifest.
Maybe this is what your miracle is waiting on.

Do Not Stop Believing

Ezekiel tells us that he spoke the message God gave him just
as it was told to him. Then he uses this word that I love:
suddenly. "Suddenly as I spoke, there was a rattling noise all
across the valley" (verse 7). See, you cannot stop speaking.
You cannot just say it one time and think you are good. No,
you have to keep speaking, keep asking and keep believing
until the manifestation comes.

Notice Ezekiel said that the "suddenly" came as he spoke
the Lord's message. It was not, "Suddenly as I was sitting
quietly," or "Suddenly while I was upset," or "Suddenly when
I was sleeping." No!

"Suddenly as I spoke, there was a rattling noise all across
the valley." Each of the bones began to rattle. Can you imagine the sound? Can you imagine the sight? Bones just rattling
and dragging themselves across the ground to reconnect with
their missing parts. A knee bone here, a shin bone there.
Bodies joining back together. A sign of unity.

If we do not come together as believers, we will never see any kind of revival sweep this world. If we do not have unity among the brothers and sisters in Christ, we will never see God move. You cannot have a strong military if its soldiers are separated. You cannot have a cohesive sports team if the players are separated. You do not need to be All Stars to win a championship—you just need to be in unity. Unity is the most powerful thing there is. In a marriage, it is unity that makes the couple strong. You can weather anything together if you have unity. Even nationally, a country will remain strong if there is unity among its people.

"Then as I watched, muscles and flesh formed over the bones. Then skin formed to cover their bodies, but they still had no breath in them" (verse 8). Now the bones were connected and looked like real people, but something was still missing. They were just shells. There was nothing in them, no life. It was like the First Zombie Assembly Church. Nothing was happening. There was no breath.

What happens to us when we feel as if life is giving us more than we can handle? We feel hopeless and disconnected from those around us. We are going through the motions of life, but we are doing it without joy or peace. We have little faith that we will be able to rise up out of the ashes.

Then God said to Ezekiel, "Speak a prophetic message to the winds, son of man" (Ezekiel 37:9). Do you see that you have to keep speaking? One time will not do. Maybe that is the problem. Maybe we are not speaking enough. Maybe we are not diligent enough to declare the Word of the Lord over our situation until it shows signs of life. Maybe we are not consistent enough. We have to be consistent in speaking a prophetic message to the winds. Speak to the winds. In Acts 2:2 it was called a mighty rushing wind.

The Power of Wind

Have you been in a hurricane or tornado? I grew up in southern Louisiana, where hurricanes and tornadoes are not rare. I have been through many hurricanes and tornadoes. A lot of times, a hurricane will spawn tornadoes in front of itself. Tornadoes come in first, kind of like destroyers around an aircraft carrier, the hurricane. Then more tornadoes follow. And the rain in these hurricanes—my friends in Modesto do not know anything about that. It rains so hard that you have to pull off the road because you cannot see the road even with your windshield wipers on high.

Hurricane winds and tornado winds have the ability to blow you out of a building. They are powerful. They are so forceful that they can uproot trees and tear down buildings. We have to speak to winds like that! Our words harness that kind of wind and put it to proper use.

God told Ezekiel to say to the winds, "This is what the Sovereign LORD says: Come, O breath, from the four winds! Breathe into these dead bodies so they may live again" (verse 9). Come, breath of heaven! Come, Holy Spirit, as You did in the valley of dry bones. Breathe on us today.

Keep Breathing

As God did, you have the ability to breathe into people. You have the ability to speak so that they live again. Just because you attend church on Sunday and Wednesday nights does not necessarily mean that you are alive. There are many dead Christians walking around. Just because you clap and lift your hands during worship does not mean that everything is great at home. Just because you get anointed with oil and go down under the Spirit does not mean your life has changed or that you have been revived. It might just mean you will have crazy hair when you get up.

As a pastor, I breathe life into the members of our local church and into the Body of Christ as I travel. My job is to do this; however, I am going to be honest. It gets frustrating to breathe life for forty years and not see many of those I invest in come to life. You understand what I am saying?

I say, "Hey, let's meet to pursue God together. Let's start a growth track. Let's do life groups. Let's get the world involved." But people sit there and say, "I ain't gonna do that. I don't have time for that. I don't wanna pray for revival. I don't have time to serve." This is why we need to be faithful when we are speaking to dead bones. We cannot stop. There are too many believers who must be dead because they are not wanting more of God. They need us to keep speaking until they come alive.

Thousands of ministers in America leave the ministry every month. They quit. Thousands. You know why? Because they keep expending all this effort and activity and they get no reaction from the people. The people are dead, so they get discouraged and leave the ministry.

What is it going to take for those who call themselves Christians to take the initiative and get on fire for themselves? It is not my job to set you on fire. I am here to breathe on you and to tell you what I believe God wants you to know. But God has a lot more in store for you than just what I can bring you. You are going to have to get serious about your relationship with God. You'll need to get serious about coming to Him and allowing Him to change you. You must want to come alive, to be revived.

A Great Army Arose

The Spirit wind came into the bodies of the dry bones that had joined back together in the valley. They all came to life. When you come to life, you stand. "They all came to life and stood up on their feet—a great army" (verse 10).

You cannot be part of a great army if you are lying down. It does no good to have a sitting army. No, you have to be on your feet and ready for battle. You have to be upright to enlist in the battle. You have to tell God, "Count me in. I am not going to sit back and watch from the sidelines. Give me a uniform, give me a gun and give me some boots. I am ready to go to war. I am tired of the devil coming at me. I am going to take the battle to him. I have had enough!"

If we are going to become a world-changing, Kingdom-advancing army, we are going to have to be in unity. We must do this together. I need your help—you need mine. When we are in this together, we will see revival come. It will not come only to us personally. It will come to our families, our churches, our communities and our nation.

Three Characteristics of the Wind

I want to talk about three specific characteristics of the wind: its ability to renew, its ability to refresh and its ability to awaken the miraculous. The wind is extraordinary. We cannot see it, but we can see everything it touches. We can see the change it makes around us. We cannot hold it in our hand, but we can feel it as it sweeps over us.

The winds of revival are more extraordinary than what we think of as wind. They are the winds of God. They are the workings of God and not of human effort. The winds are the breath of His voice, that life-giving voice that took our empty shells and made us alive.

Imagine the feeling of a cool wind on a scorching hot summer day. It rushes over you and revives you. It dries the sweat, and for a moment, it takes away the memory of toil. This is the way the wind of revival refreshes you. It is the deep breath you need to keep moving forward in this life.

The wind carries the voice of God. When God speaks, the whole earth hears. When He speaks, revival comes. No other voice can do that. That is why His breath is extraordinary, unbelievable.

The wind of revival is God's voice to a broken heart. It speaks the words that need to be said to a heart in full surrender. It declares the Word of God and causes dry bones to come alive once again. You will not see the wind of revival, but you will surely feel its miracle work inside you and see its effect in your life as hope is renewed, faith is renewed and God is pursued.

Trust me—when you feel God touch you, when you see God kiss your family, your community and your city, you will be amazed beyond words. It will be unmistakable that He is doing something unbelievable in your midst.

Revival is a move of God, not man. We cannot produce this ourselves. We are not good enough to produce this ourselves. All we can do is what God tells us to do. Our obedience brings us into alignment, but it is God who revives us. If God does not act, we will never be revived. That is why we pray, and that is why we praise. Those are landing strips for God to come down and meet us.

I wonder if the Spirt of God has been flying all over our nation looking for a place He can land. I believe He wants to show up and explode. I believe He wants to blow the prison doors open like He did for Paul and Silas (see Acts 16:25–26). Maybe He will blow the doors of your home open and friends and neighbors will come in to get a taste of what God is doing in your midst. Hallelujah!

When Revival Comes

The God of the Bible is also the God of revival, and we must refuse to let God go until He blesses us with it. I do not want Him to leave until He touches me.

It is amazing to me that people can go to church and notice that Jim's hairstyle has changed or look at the design on Sally's fingernails and yet never hear part of the message that is preached from the pulpit. How we can get distracted! Let me just say this: When revival comes, an intense spirit of conviction will be felt immediately. Churches will reel as those who called themselves believers see where they really are in their walk with Christ. People who have no intention of becoming Christians will get radically saved, because true revival brings extraordinary results.

When revival comes, conduct that has always seemed acceptable will appear unbelievably wicked.

When revival comes, prejudices will be revealed as sins in your life.

When revival comes, hate against others will not be tolerated anymore.

When revival comes, private indulgences that a person has looked at as being okay will suddenly be considered offensive to God.

When revival comes, prayerlessness, ignorance of Scripture, sins of omission and failure of good works will no longer be defended by a pocket-full of excuses.

When revival comes, pride and self-centered living will no longer be excused.

When revival comes, words carefully spoken will rise from forgotten graves and bring a wave of conviction upon you.

When revival comes, long-forgotten sins against the Body of Christ will be remembered with great grief, and believers will be restored.

When revival comes, conviction will arrive so powerfully that people who once thought themselves worthy of heaven will stand in wonder and amazement that they are not already burning in the fires of hell.

When revival comes, men and women will not be able to tolerate wickedness, and they will cry out to God to save them from their sin.

It is an awesome, awful condition when revival comes. The cross of Jesus Christ, which had seemed very distant, becomes very real when revival comes. The price that was paid for us carries more weight in our hearts when revival comes. We will want more of God. We need more of God anyway, do we not?

Where Is Your Awe?

Can I ask, where is your awe of God today? Where is the awe? Awe is short for awesome. I am filled with awe over God. Have you forgotten who He is? He is pretty awesome.

He is pretty unbelievable. Maybe you have lost that awe and you have been taking Him for granted. Maybe that is why you are not being generous and giving of your resources and time. Maybe you have lost your first love.

I love talking to new believers because they try so hard to describe what happened to them when they got saved. "I don't know. I was just lost. I have been bound, but all of a sudden, I feel free. I don't know what happened to me, but it is the greatest feeling I have ever had!" It is just unbelievable to them, and they are filled with wonder over it. God is so great! God, give my friend a fresh awe of You.

You have to do more than just talk. You must obey and do good. What is it going to take to get you to do what God wants you to do? If you want revival to come, you need to start crying out for God to move. Start repeating the things you have been taught to say because you need God's Spirit.

Nothing is going to change your family. Nothing is going to change you. Nothing is going to restore your home. Nothing is going to bring your prodigal child home. Nothing is going to get rid of the drugs. Nothing is going to break for anyone other than God. God has to come. He has to breathe on you. He has to do a miracle work and perform the supernatural for you. God has to come!

Time to Make a Move

God is waiting for you, and you are waiting for God, and God is waiting for you. It is going to be an endless cycle. You have to ask yourself if you want revival. Do you really want it, or do you want to live this life half-heartedly? You wonder why Christianity has not worked for you the way it has worked for others. When another's life is blessed, it is because they are all in. You have to be all in. It is time to make a move. God is ready and waiting. He is ready for your heart to be aligned with His will and to reflect His priorities.

Say this with me: I am all in, God. I want You. I am making You first place in every area of my life. No more mediocrity. No more lukewarmness. I know complacency breeds complacency. I will not let my heart be a boulder of resistance. I surrender to You today.

If you need to ask God to forgive you for something, do so right now. You know you are not where you need to be. Just be honest about it. You know you are better than where you are right now. You have been living below where God has called you to live. That can change today.

Revival brings repentance. It convicts our hearts. Do not run from it; allow what God is doing. It is Jesus. If God showed up, you would immediately feel conviction in the areas of your life that are not lining up with Him. The more God comes, the more you are going to want to get rid of the wrong things in your life. This is wonderful.

I will tell you this, until I got saved, I never lived. I thought I was alive and thought I had it all together, and then I realized how messed up I really was. I only started to live after I was saved.

Right where you are, pray this with me.

Lord Jesus, forgive me of the sins hindering me from my personal revival. Come into my life afresh. You died for me when I was a sinner. You loved me before I loved You, but now I am a new creation and I want revival. I want everything You have for me. I do not want to be apathetic anymore. Lethargy has no place in my life. Put a fire in my spirit. I release the wind, the breath of

God, the Spirit of God to blow the trash in my life to hell. Let me stand before You in the newness of my spiritual life. I am coming back to You, Father. In Jesus' name, Amen.

The winds of God are going to revive you. You will never be able to go back to the way things were. Moving forward, you will need to fight to get into the presence of God in your home and at church. You are going to be early to church. You are going to make sure you are praying and pursuing God daily and become involved in godly things. Why? Because you want to be part of what God is doing. You want revival!

As you press into Him, He will show you what you need to do. But the first step is to give everything to Him. Get all in. Everything changes when you recognize Him as supreme in your life. Whatever He wants is His, and what He wants most of all is your completely surrendered heart. Give yourself to Him in every way and watch revival winds blow in your life.

9 | How to Have a Fire Revival

I came back from ministering in Australia some time ago with revival on my mind. The Lord showed me the reason we do not have earth-shaking revivals is because we are content to live without Him. That sounds harsh, but it is true. We do not necessarily care about revival. We do not care if we have revival or not. It does not matter. Our mindset too often is, "Let's just go to church. I wanna feel better. That's all I really want, nothing else."

You know what I think of my nation? I think it needs a revival. I think America needs revived cities. I think we have gone in a downward spiral. Things are not looking so good here. I do not think I am telling you something you do not know. America is in a downward spiral in every area of society, and we are more divided than we have ever been before. That is why we need revival. Right now. In this season. It is not going to come from any source but God. It has to come through the Body of Christ. It has to come from us, but it cannot until we have a personal revival.

Imagine with me a group of revived believers, all sorts of different people, going around their cities and speaking the same word with the same excitement. Their cities would hear the truth about Christ. They would understand that Jesus is the answer to every challenge we are facing. He is the hope, and He is the peace in the midst of the chaos this world creates. If we all took part in this revival together, nations could be revolutionized. I know it is a dream, but I believe that dreams can become reality.

Needed Consequences

In Judges 13, we read about Samson. Before Samson was born, the Israelites were doing evil in the Lord's sight. Because of this, He handed them over to Philistine oppression for forty years. This should cause you to stop and think. When you do evil or sin against God, consequences come. Consequences are not necessarily the devil's doing. Maybe they are your own fault! Maybe the Lord has turned you over to the devil.

Maybe He is tired of your foolishness.

Maybe He is tired of your rebellion.

Maybe He is tired of trying to reach out to you.

Maybe He is tired of the way you have been acting.

Maybe He is trying to get you right again.

Maybe He is trying to reach out and pull you back.

Maybe He is tired of you rejecting Him, not giving, not going to church, not praying and not reading your Bible.

Maybe it is good He turns you over. Maybe it is about time He turns you over. Maybe this is a wake-up call for you to straighten up. I know it would be for me because I do not want God to leave me. I do not want to go a day without His presence in my life.

The State of Things

Israel was oppressed for forty years. Some say forty is an interesting amount. It is found 146 times in the Bible, and it symbolizes testing, trials and probation. Let me give you some forties here:

Moses lived in the desert for forty years. He was on Mount Sinai receiving God's Law for forty days and forty nights on two different occasions.

The Israelites wandered around the wilderness for forty years, and the spies went into the Promised Land for forty days.

God flooded the earth for forty days and forty nights.

The Old Testament judges governed for forty years.

The first three kings—Saul, David and Solomon—each ruled for forty years.

Jonah warned Nineveh about impending doom for forty days.

The prophet Ezekiel laid on his right side for forty days, symbolizing Judah's sin.

Elijah went without food and water on Mount Horeb for forty days.

Jesus was tempted by the devil forty days and forty nights. He was resurrected and appeared to

His disciples for forty days before ascending to heaven.

You know what, the Bible is written by forty different writers. These are only a few of the 146 biblical references to the significance of number forty!

It seems as if it is a daily occurrence that we hear stories in which Christians are put down, disrespected because of what they believe, and have their values threatened to be removed from the laws of our nation. We are almost at a point where the agenda of the enemies of God is no longer a secret. They are open about their intentions. They are almost daring us, as the Body of Christ, "Let's see what you got! What are you going to do about it? How are you going to fight back?"

Here are some things that have happened in America:

A girl at a freshman orientation at a state university was told to remove or hide her cross necklace because it would offend some students.[1]

A middle school student was entering his classroom in the back of the line. A longtime substitute teacher said, "The first shall be last and the last shall be first." The student asked, "Where did you get that phrase from?" The teacher showed him where the verse was found in his Bible and gave him his Bible. The teacher was fired by the school district.[2]

A second-grade student was told she could not sing her favorite song, "Awesome God," in an after-school talent show.[3]

A Florida professor told a student to write the name of Jesus on a sheet of paper and put it on the floor, and everybody got up and stomped on it.[4]

Senior citizens in Port Wentworth, Georgia, were told they could not pray before meals because it violated the separation of church and state because the food came from a federal funding program.[5]

An Illinois high school valedictorian was told minutes before his graduation speech to remove all religious references that mentioned God or Jesus.[6]

The United States Armed Forces blocked access to the Southern Baptist Convention website at many bases because it contained what they deemed to be hostile content.[7]

A little girl, ten years old, and her classmates were assigned to pick one idol to write about, and the little girl picked God. This is what she wrote: "God is my idol. He will always be the number-one person I look up to. God is the reason I'm on this earth. I love Him and Jesus." She was told by her teacher that she was to start over because she could not use God as an idol for her assignment.[8]

How can you have separation of church and state when our constitution mentions God? In California, where I have lived for many years, we have this preamble to our constitution: "We, the people of the State of California, grateful to Almighty God for our freedom, in order to secure and perpetuate its blessings, do establish this Constitution."[9] We have God written in marble in Washington, D. C.: "In God we trust." Why are we trying to remove God from every American constitution?

Over the past 25 years, I have watched America become a nation that God cannot bless. "The land of the free and the home of the brave" has become, "The land of me and the home of the bound." Our slogan, "In God we trust" has been changed to, "In nothing I trust." Words like *virginity*, *integrity* and *hard work* are now in the history books of past American values. As I travel the world, I find the same to be true in other nations. There is an organized, relentless extermination of Christian influence, values and rights that is taking place globally.

The demise of moral, social and economic structures has not been because of the ACLU. It has not been because of drug pushers, abortionists, crooked politicians, homosexuals, agnostic judges, atheistic organizations, pornography or Hollywood music. Although that is a motley crew, the Bible does not only say that sin brings reproach to a nation, it also says righteousness exalts a nation. If we would just get some righteousness in here!

It is time that we as believers stand up and stop taking whatever is thrown our way. I am not taking it any longer because I know that when the church lights are shut off, the devil is going to turn his on. I will not let that happen on my watch!

There was a Great Awakening many years ago. American universities like Harvard and Yale, all the Ivy League schools, were Christian universities. The Reformation came and stirred Europe. It brought revival to America one hundred years ago. It was a scream that awakened a nation. It was also the launching of the pentecostal spirit that covered our whole anemic country at the time. It is time for another revival to sweep your nation. Amen?

The Angel and the Fire

Back to Samson. When Samson was strong, the nation was strong. The Philistine enemies of Israel were not a threat while Samson was there. No food? No water? No problem while Samson was strong. The success of Israel was the success of Samson. He was God's anointed person. I believe there is something we need to learn from the history of Samson as it relates to us today.

Samson's ability to bring revival to Israel was not without conditions, and they are the same conditions that we must meet today if we are to see a prophetic move of God come to pass. Samson's father was wise and knew the conditions. When God puts His hand on a man or a woman, that individual will have two responsibilities: to be what God has called him to be and to do what God has called him to do. Every person who has ever made a difference has had to start with this same understanding.

Here is Samson's story (see Judges 13). In the days of the Israelite oppression, a man named Manoah lived in a town called Zorah. His wife was unable to become pregnant, so they had no children.

The angel of the Lord appeared to Manoah's wife. Why did he appear to the wife? Because men do not listen! Why did the devil appear to Eve? Why go after her? Because he went after the influence. The wife represents influence, and the man represents authority. The man is the head, but the woman is the neck. It turns the head, right?

So the angel of the Lord appeared to the wife and not to Manoah. He would not have believed right away. The woman believed. And his message to her was, "Even though you have been unable to have children, you will soon become pregnant and give birth to a son" (Judges 13:3). If you are struggling to have a child, grieving the loss of a child or believing for a child, write Judges 13:3–4 down and claim it. If God could cause a barren man and woman to conceive a child back then, He can do it again today.

The angel went on, "Be careful; you must not drink wine or any other alcoholic drink nor eat forbidden food. You will become pregnant and give birth to a son, and his hair must never be cut" (Judges 13:4–5). So in case you did not know why Samson could not cut his hair, it was because he had been dedicated to God as a Nazirite. The Nazirites were a group of Jews who voluntarily took a vow to abstain from drinking alcohol, who avoided anything that had perished and who refrained from cutting their hair. He was destined to rescue Israel from the enemies of God, the Philistines.

The woman ran and told her husband that an angel had appeared to her and that he was terrifying looking. Anytime you hear a preacher or somebody on television talk flippantly about angels, he or she did not really see an angel. If someone says, "The other day I woke in the middle of night and two angels were standing at the foot of my bed. They said they were hungry, so I got up and made some food for them. We sat down and enjoyed a nice meal together and some iced tea and talked about the Bible. After that, they disappeared, and I went back to sleep," odds are that he or she had a bad taco. I am just telling you. There is no time in the Bible when people see an angel, a supernatural being, and are okay with it. They are always terrified and surprised.

Some people act so spiritual. They brag about flying around and living with angelic encounters. "I was just with angels the other day." No, they are crazy. That is not true.

Manoah's wife said, "He told me I will become pregnant and give birth to a son." Manoah heard her story and prayed to God, saying, "Lord, please let the man of God come back and tell me, because I don't believe my wife!" What is wrong with you, man? Come on!

God answered Manoah's prayer, and the Lord appeared once again to his wife who was sitting in the field by herself. She ran quickly and told her husband, "The man who appeared to me the other day is here again!" (Judges 13:10). Wow! He came back!

Manoah went to the angel and said, "Are you the man who spoke to my wife the other day about the kid we are going to have?"

He replied, "Yes, I am."

And Manoah asked the angel, "Will you please stay here until we can prepare young goats for you to eat?"

"Yes, I will stay," he said. "You may prepare a burnt offering and sacrifice it to the Lord."

Anytime God does something for you, you need to give a sacrifice. That is the Bible. If God does something for you and you do not give a sacrifice, do not expect God to do anything else. Sacrificing is just part of what you do when God blesses you. You bless God again. Say you just got one thousand dollars. You should not keep the thousand dollars and give a verbal *thank you*. No, that is going to be the last thousand you get. You better give a sacrifice. I am just reading the Bible here (see 1 Kings 3:3–5; Hebrews 13:15–16; Malachi 3:10).

Manoah asked the angel, "What is your name? For when all this comes true, we want to honor you" (Judges 13:17).

The angel replied, "Why do you ask my name? It is too wonderful for you to understand" (see verse 18). I want you to think a minute. Whose name is wonderful? Gabriel is not called wonderful. Michael is not called wonderful. Jesus is. So the angel of the Lord was Jesus. He is right here in the Old Testament.

Then Manoah took a young goat and some grain and offered it as a sacrifice to the Lord. His wife watched, and "the LORD did an amazing thing" (verse 19). As the fire shot up toward the sky, the angel ascended in the fire. This was similar to Elijah's ascension to heaven. Manoah and his wife fell with their faces to the ground when they saw this spectacle.

The problem with most of us is that we have heard the Word taught, but we have not seen the supernatural fire of God. If we are going to have revival, if we are going to deal with the agnostics, atheists and humanists, if we are going to make a difference in this world, we need the supernatural fire of Almighty God.

Send the Fire

God wants to send fire into your life. You have been dead long enough. You have been trying in your own strength long enough. It is time for you to see something you have never seen before that rocks your life and leaves you on your face.

The fire consumes your doubt. It consumes your disbelief. It consumes your fear. If you saw supernatural fire, it would totally change you. Manoah could doubt his wife, he could doubt the angelic messenger, but he could not doubt the fire.

We often become pragmatic about things. In our pragmatism, we become powerless. We have believers who meet together and think they are powerful because of the size of their churches. That is not God's way. We are not powerful without the power of God being evident in our lives.

Sometimes your thirst for something new is really just a substitute for the fact that you do not have a genuine relationship with God, or you are not clear about what He wants for your life. The Bible says that the letter of the law kills, but the Spirit of God gives life (see 2 Corinthians 3:6). The fire of God gives life.

The presence and power of God always come with supernatural fire. It happened in Exodus 3 when Moses was standing at the burning bush. Without it, he could have never challenged Pharaoh. During Elijah's fiery showdown on Mount Carmel, the prophets of Baal witnessed the supernatural fire of God that fell (see 1 Kings 18). Elisha witnessed his master depart in a chariot of fire drawn by horses that were on fire (see 2 Kings 2). In Isaiah 6, the angel touched Isaiah's mouth with the flaming coals from the altar and purged his sin, causing him to shout out, "Lord, here I am! Use me!" Jeremiah said God's words were like "fire in my bones" (Jeremiah 20:9). As the Church prayed for forty days, cloven tongues of fire fell on their heads, and they left the Upper Room and changed the world (see Acts 2).

We need fire! When you have the fire of God, you can hear the simplest thing like "Jesus saves," and you get excited about it. You think back to how He saved you. It does not matter how long you have been saved. You think back to the very beginning of your walk with Jesus when you heard His voice and felt the fire of God touch you. Then a supernatural peace came over your life. A person who is on fire can remember these things and overflow with happiness.

The fire of God consumes your past failures. The fire confirms the Word of God in your life. There was no other confirmation needed for Manoah concerning Samson other than the supernatural fire of God. I am sure as Samson was growing up, his father told him, "Son, you're special. You have a calling. I know because there was a supernatural fire and the man who told me about you walked into the fire and went up to heaven right before my eyes."

If you need a confirmation of God's will for your life, get in your prayer closet, alone, on your face, without your phone, and seek God. He wants to show you some supernatural fire because you have been walking along living a mediocre faith life long enough. It is time for you to get passionate, to get on fire and to start doing something for Him.

You know what happens when you see an angel do something supernatural? You start thinking, "I'm gonna die! I'm dead!" John fell on his face as if dead when he saw the supernatural (see Revelation 1:17). It makes me wonder how many Christians today have really had an experience with God. Most have never even been in awe of Him, let alone thought they were going to die. It is critically important that we experience the God who brings the fire. We must have a revelation of who He really is and the power that comes with His presence.

I am convinced that the only way we can remove the garbage from our lives for good is to burn it with supernatural fire.

I am convinced that criticism, gossip, anger and foul language will only be purged from our lips by supernatural fire. I am tired of hearing profanity on television. I am tired of hearing profanity in every movie. I am tired of people flippantly throwing words around. We have dropped so low in our society that we do not care what anybody thinks anymore.

I am convinced that the only way we are going to destroy doubt, discouragement and depression is with the supernatural fire of God.

I am convinced that the only way we will experience nation-shaking revival is by a heaven-sent supernatural fire. It is not going to be from better preaching, it is not going to be from better music and it is not going to be from better facilities. Send the fire, Lord! Send the fire. Our nations need a fire revival.

What This World Needs

There was a time in American history when the Church elected the politicians. Some of us who are older can remember it. We legislated laws based on Scripture. I know it is hard to believe now, but that is the way it used to be. Pastors controlled the violence in communities more than the police did. While the deviants would fight the police, they would not touch the men of God. Because of this, pastors walked arm-in-arm down the streets saying, "Go back home," and the bad guys would go back home.

The Church dictated the spiritual climate in the cities of America. Now American cities are filled with violence, crime, pollution, drugs, gangs and pornography. And the Church is hiding its head in the sand.

What if we decided to be part of a supernatural body of believers that was determined to face and beat the enemy? It is time to put away our petty differences. It is time to give up our time-consuming hobbies. It is time to distance ourselves from the sins that so easily ensnare us.

It is time for us to stand like fire-breathing disciples, declaring to our hopeless society that there is hope. Hope is not found in psychology. We have tried that. It is not found in education. We have tried that. It is not found in counseling. We have tried that. It is not found in medical research.

We have tried that, too. There is hope, but it is only found in believers who are on fire for Jesus Christ and who are ready at His command.

I am ready for the devil to say, "I give up." It is time for the devil to surrender your life and your family. You have put up with his buffeting long enough. Get the fire of God and get some grit in your life.

I would like to find some shoulder pads that fit you and put a football jersey on you. Before you know it, I am going to get your head sized for a helmet to put you in the game. You have been sitting by and watching too long. You have been watching everybody else play. You have been hearing everybody else's stories. You do not get a story until you get on the field. You cannot be a champion if you do not get into the battle.

If you are not from America, what about in your country? What is the spiritual climate? Where are you as the Body of Christ? I am telling you, you can face and beat the enemy. You can declare over your society the hope found only in Jesus Christ. Ask the Lord how you can get into the battle and take back your land.

What Will You Do for God?

One day, God is going to look at you and He is going to say, "What did you do for Me?" Will you say, "Well, I heard a lot, but I didn't really serve or try to make a difference because I was pretty busy. I had my job and hobbies and friends, and my car needed work done." Is the car going to be with you in heaven? No, it is not going to be there. But what you do for God is going to be told in heaven. Those people you lead to Christ will be in heaven. You can be complacent or cowardly, or you can stand up and start being a champion for God.

The city of Nineveh was comprised of 600,000 people—and they were all saved in one revival! There is no reason why the city you are living in cannot be saved. Unfortunately, we are often too comfortable in our routines and are not serving in church or reaching out to our community. In case you did not know, Jesus did not hang around with religious people much. He went out to the lost people where there were needs.

When we get outside the church, we will see how able we are to make a difference. Remember how, before you were saved, you thought you were all that? Then when you got saved, you realized how stupid you were? I know I did some stupid things. I was brainless back in the world. I did not have any sense at all. I got saved, and all of a sudden, I got smarter. We cannot forget this. We cannot forget that the world is stuck in a cycle of sin, and only we have the answer to get them unstuck.

But how do we make a difference? We need supernatural fire. You may have had fire back in the day, and because of the challenges of life, you got sidelined or distracted. It is time to pray and seek the face of God to rekindle the flame within you.

Do you want more of God? Are you satisfied where you are spiritually? I have been saved for more than 45 years, and I am more excited today to see God move than I have ever been. The fire is not supposed to die out as you grow in Christ. It is supposed to grow bigger and stronger. The more it grows, the more the devil will have to stay away from you. He will not want to take you on because you will be too strong for him! It would be easier for him to go looking for some wobbly Christian who cannot get their footing.

You will touch your city when you get fed up with the world. When you have had it with your past, with your sin, with the issues of life that seem to creep up and put you in chains—that is when the fire of God will fall on you. Do not be satisfied with where you are today. God has more in store for you.

DO NOT BE SATISFIED WITH WHERE YOU ARE TODAY. GOD HAS MORE IN STORE FOR YOU.

If you have been complacent in your walk, I encourage you to take a moment and simply pray. Ask God to cleanse your heart with His supernatural fire. Ask Him to remove everyone and everything that is hindering you. Then commit to Him that you are going to care about what He thinks more than what people think. You are going to let your light shine. Pray this prayer with me:

Set me ablaze, Lord. Today I choose You over everything in my life. Help me finish the race You have called me to, and help me reach this world for Christ!

I am with you in this. There is unity between you and me. Together, we are going to fight the devil for our nations and for the world. He cannot mess with us. With God all things are possible. Hallelujah!

10 | How to Have a Power Revival

If I knew I was going to die and had only one message left to preach, I think I would aim for it to be the best message of my life. I would try to make my most important statement something that I would want remembered for the ages. For this reason, it would be wise of us to pay special attention to the last messages Jesus shared. He knew His time was coming to an end, and He must have wanted to give us critical information while He had the opportunity.

Consider when Jesus told His disciples that wherever they went in the world, they should share the Good News (see Mark 16:15–17). He said, "Anyone who believes and is baptized will be saved. But anyone who refuses to believe will be condemned" (verse 16).

We were vacationing one year and stopped at a restaurant to eat. God told me something specific about the life of our waitress. I revealed that to her. It so touched her that by the time we left the restaurant, she had repented through tears. Jesus said that wherever we go, we are to be the light of the world. You cannot just let your light shine among Christians—there is no darkness in the Church. You have to get outside the walls of your local body. Darkness is everywhere out there. Tell everyone, tell everyone, tell everyone.

Jesus said we are to tell everyone the Good News and to baptize those who believe so that they will be saved. And then He tells us, "These miraculous signs will accompany those who believe: They will cast out demons in my name, and they will speak in new languages" (verse 17). Miraculous signs. If you believe in Jesus, there should be some miraculous things happening around you that point people to Jesus. You should have stories about what God has done and is doing in your life. They will convey the power and authority of the name of Jesus. His name is a powerful name.

Jesus told the disciples that He was sending them what His Father had promised (see Luke 24:49). They only needed to wait in the city until they received power from heaven. What was that power the Father had promised? It was the Holy Spirit, our Comforter to be with us in place of Jesus in the flesh.

I think it is interesting to note that Jesus said it was going to be better for us that He left. I am sure the disciples disagreed. What could be better that having God with you in human form? What could be more powerful than witnessing signs and wonders at the hands of Jesus up close and personal? But Jesus was in the flesh, so He could only be at one place at one time. When He was in Capernaum, He could not be in Galilee. But the Holy Spirit can be in both places—in all places—all at once. After Jesus returned to heaven, the disciples received the Holy Spirit, which allowed them to spread the Gospel and perform signs and wonders everywhere they went.

What I love about Luke's retelling of Jesus' last message is that he says in verse 51 that while Jesus was blessing them, "he left them and was taken up to heaven" (verse 51). What a sermon close that would be! Imagine that: I preach my last message, and as I preach, I float to heaven with trumpets and angels. The angels are playing the guitar and the harp, and they are singing, "Hosanna! Welcome home, Glen!" That is what I see when I close my eyes. I do not know if it really went that way but would that not be a nice close at the end of a sermon?! It would be nice.

You would think if someone did that in closing their message, you would really pay attention to what they had said. But do you realize that out of the five hundred people who heard Him clearly say, "Wait here," only 120 obeyed? That is right. There were 380 of them who did not go to the Upper Room.

This makes me wonder. If Jesus was speaking to you today and said it was His last message and that He was ascending to heaven, would you listen to what He said? Or would you go get some chimichangas afterward?

The biggest problem we have as people is we love to say things, but we struggle to do them. Jesus did not say, "Well said, good and faithful servant." He said, "Well done," right? I do not care about what you say. People say a lot of things. Just look at Facebook, Twitter or Instagram. We say a lot, but our walks are measured by what we do. Unfortunately, we do not do much of what we say.

Jesus had given His chosen apostles instructions. He received His orders from the Holy Spirit, and then He passed those orders on to His disciples. He depended on the Holy Spirit, and He tried to explain to His disciples that the cross and the resurrection were not to finish anything; they were to begin something that would be carried out by the Holy Spirit at work in and through us.

Jesus was saying, "If you think you and I have had some good times over our three and a half years together, oh, it's just starting, baby! We're just getting ready to go on this adventure. This thing has not even happened yet. I want to give you a new Spirit. I want to give you a power Spirit. With this Spirit, you can bring revival to your towns, your cities, your nation and the world."

A Baptism of Power

"After his death Jesus showed the apostles a lot of convincing evidence that he was alive. For 40 days he appeared to them and talked with them about God's kingdom" (Acts 1:3 GW). God's Kingdom means God's way of doing things. He ordered His disciples not to leave Jerusalem but to wait there for the Holy Spirit to come.

Jesus said to them, "John baptized with water, but in a few days you will be baptized with the Holy Spirit" (Acts 1:5 GW). Anytime you see John's baptism with water mentioned, it signifies repentance (see Acts 19:4).

John the Baptist was a repentance preacher, but the baptism of the Holy Spirit is a baptism of power. We are a powerless group of people. God says that we need the power of the Holy Spirit in our lives (see Romans 15:13).

We have enough instruction. We have enough preaching. We have enough information. We have enough access to the Bible. We have enough meetings. We have enough church meetings. What we need is power, and that power can only come from the baptism of the Holy Spirit.

Jesus said, "You will receive it." That means they did not have it before that point. "But," He said, "the only way you're going to get it is by being My witnesses."

Did you know that people who have demonic spirits are spreading the news about their drugs use, their alcohol consumption, and how many people they have slept with? But you and I, with the Holy Spirit inside us, do not spread the news about Jesus. We hide in a closet. While everybody in the world is coming out of the closet, we are going in to hide.

I think this is why Jesus said that after we receive power, "Then you will be my witnesses to testify about me in Jerusalem, throughout Judea and Samaria, and to the ends of the earth" (Acts 1:8 GW). Jesus was talking about everywhere. He said all this, and then He was taken to heaven. Poof! He floats up to heaven. A cloud hid Him. They could not see Him any longer.

Of the people who watched Jesus disappear into the clouds, many of them, 380 disciples, watched that happen and then turned to each other and said, "That was different. Let's have lunch." Seriously. They did not do anything. And just so you know, you never hear about the 380 again in the Bible. You only read about the 120 who did as Jesus commanded. The others did not receive the power.

Led by the Spirit

In Matthew 4:1, we read that the Holy Spirit led Jesus into the wilderness to be tempted of the devil. God used the Holy Spirit to lead Jesus. He was led by the Spirit. The Holy Spirit was the channel of direct contact between Jesus and God.

In the wilderness when the devil tried to tempt Jesus, what kept Him from sinning was the power of the Holy Spirit in His life. He was able to reject sin. One of the jobs of the Holy Spirit is to keep you from sinning. He gives you the power to stay pure, the power to stay holy.

When the disciples received the Holy Spirit, they did not have the weakness that plagued them before. Their weakness was no longer there.

We never read about Doubting Thomas after Pentecost because he never doubted again. He never questioned. He died preaching Jesus.

We do not read of the apostle Paul backsliding, rededicating his life and then backsliding again. You know why? Because the Holy Spirit came into his life and started working in him to keep him from sinning.

The rooster never crowed again to wake Peter up from his compromise of denying Christ during his fireside chat. Peter actually wrote that, "God opposes the proud but gives grace to the humble" (1 Peter 5:5).

The woman who had five problems—I mean five husbands —met Jesus at the well and never thirsted again. She was led by the Spirit. She was codependent no longer.

We never see the traveling evangelist Philip having an adultery problem, a lust problem or an issue with women. The power of the Holy Spirit kept him from sinning.

With his great intellect, Nicodemus never again questioned the born-again experience.

The prostitute, Mary Magdalene, did not go back into the world and sleep around with men because the Holy Spirit was now operating in her life.

Tree-climbing Zacchaeus did not have to climb another tree after he received the Holy Spirit.

If Jesus needed the Holy Spirit, what makes you think you do not? Who are you?

Power to Live Holy

The power of the Holy Spirit can keep you holy, righteous and conquering sin.

> Just think how much more the blood of Christ will purify our consciences from sinful deeds so that we can worship the living God. For by the power of the eternal [Holy] Spirit, Christ offered himself to God as a perfect sacrifice for our sins.
>
> Hebrews 9:14

This is proof. The Holy Spirit helped Jesus not to sin and helped Him to be perfect. What is the Holy Spirit? Power.

Some people cry, "I can't believe I keep going back to my same old ways. I just can't make it! I just can't be a Christian. I'm powerless!" But Jesus says that because of the Holy Spirit, He was able to live a perfect life. What are you able to do with that same power? By the way, did you know the Holy Spirit has a first name? It is Holy. That is His name. Holy. Set apart. Sacred.

I want you to remember the disciples before the Holy Spirit came. They were weak. They were afraid. They were timid. They were fearful. They were unproductive. They had information. They had methodology. They had practical ministry experience watching Jesus. They had hands-on experience, but they had no power to perform anything.

How many people did Peter lead to the Lord before Jesus died? Zero. What happened the first day he received the Holy Spirit? He led three thousand to the Lord. Pretty good jump in power, right? If that does not show you the difference, I am not sure anything will.

When the Holy Spirit hits you, it hits you like a lightning bolt. Suddenly you are full and have the power to perform in any area God wants you to. Without the Holy Spirit, you might as well be a good-looking car with this big, five-hundred-horsepower motor that has no battery. You just sit there.

"Can you start it up?"

"It doesn't start."

I wonder how many times God has put a key in your life, but you have not moved. It is time you get moving. It is time the key turns over and the engine powers up.

When the disciples were filled and equipped with the Holy Spirit, they started speaking in tongues. Then Peter got up to speak. His sermon is something interesting to me. After the Holy Spirit fell, they were all filled and equipped for ministry. Peter stood up and declared:

"God raised Jesus from the dead, and we are all witnesses of this. Now he is exalted to the place of highest honor in heaven, at God's right hand. And the Father, as he had promised, gave him the Holy Spirit to pour out upon us, just as you see and hear today."

Acts 2:32–33

To whom did God promise the Holy Spirit? Was it just for those who were alive at that time? You are going to hear from some pulpits that the Holy Spirit was only for those who lived two thousand years ago in Jerusalem. Some preachers believe that this gift is not for us today. They will say it was a onetime event, not something that is ongoing and for us as believers. But Acts tells us that this promise is for us today. It says, "For God's promise of the Holy Spirit is for you and your families, for those yet to be born and for everyone whom the Lord our God calls to himself" (verse 2:39 TPT).

God promised the Holy Spirit to you and your family. If you are saved and alive today, you can have the exact same Spirit that the disciples received in the Upper Room in the book of Acts.

An Outbreak of Power Revival

I was raised a Catholic. It is amazing how we can remember, "Hail Mary, full of grace, the Lord is with thee. Blessed art thou among women, and blessed is the fruit of thy womb, Jesus. Holy Mary, Mother of God, pray for us sinners now, and at the hour of our death. Amen." Right? That is right. I am a true Catholic.

We were so Catholic in South Louisiana—this is true; I am not making this up—that we had bumper stickers you could put on your car that said, "If you can't find Jesus, look for His mother." Look, a mom knows where her kid is. Seriously.

But let's just see: Where was Mary on the day of Pentecost? She had joined the apostles in the Upper Room. So had some of the other women who followed Jesus and Jesus' brothers. Together, with a single purpose, they all devoted themselves to prayer.

One year later, after Pentecost, the apostles in Jerusalem heard about people in Samaria accepting God's message, so they sent Peter and John there. And as soon as they arrived, they prayed for the new believers (and those who were already believers) to receive something called the Holy Spirit.

The Bible says that the Holy Spirit had not yet come upon any of them. They had only been baptized in the name of the Lord Jesus, which signified repentance. Then Peter and John laid their hands on them. It is all in the Bible. Do not be afraid of it. There should be no question about whether or not somebody can lay hands on me and pray for me to receive the Holy Spirit.

Do you remember the story of Saul's conversion to Paul? This took place years after Pentecost. Ananias found the house in which Saul was staying. He went inside and laid his hands on Saul. Ananias said, "The Lord Jesus, who appeared to you on the road, has sent me so that you might regain your sight and be filled with the Holy Spirit" (Acts 9:17). Saul got saved when he got knocked off his horse, but he was filled to overflowing with the Holy Spirit when Ananias laid hands on him and prayed for him.

As Saul received the Holy Spirit, His power brought back Saul's sight. Who would have thought you could get the Holy Spirit and a miracle at the same time. The power caused the substance over Saul's eyes to disappear, and he could see perfectly. Immediately, he got up and was baptized.

Seven years after Pentecost, we read that as Peter was speaking, the Holy Spirit fell upon everyone listening to him (see Acts 10:44–47). That included the Jewish believers who came with Peter and the Gentiles to the meeting. The Bible tells us that the Jewish believers were amazed that the gift of the Holy Spirit was poured out on the Gentiles (see verse 45). They thought it was only for them; however, God said, "I am going to pour it out on everyone who wants it."

How did the Jewish believers know the Gentiles had received the baptism of the Holy Spirit? Because Acts tells us, "They heard them speaking in other tongues and praising

God" (verse 46). They heard them. You see, the Bible tells us time and time again that the evidence of the infilling of the Holy Spirit is the evidence of speaking in tongues. You might not believe it, but it is very obvious in Scripture.

Born or Baptized?

There is a difference between being born in the Spirit and being baptized in the Spirit. We are born in the Spirit with evidence of our salvation and baptized in the Spirit with evidence of speaking in other tongues.

Peter asked the Jewish believers, "Can anyone object to their being baptized, now that they have received the Holy Spirit just as we did?" (Acts 10:47).

In the next chapter, Peter also says, "As I began to speak . . . the Holy Spirit fell on them, just as he fell on us at the beginning. Then I thought of the Lord's words when he said, 'John baptized with water, but you will be baptized with the Holy Spirit'" (Acts 11:15–16).

One last mention. Paul was traveling to Ephesus where he found several believers (see Acts 19:1–6). He asked them if they had received the Holy Spirit when they made Christ Lord of their lives. "'No,' they replied, 'we haven't even heard that there is a Holy Spirit'" (Acts 19:2). They had only been baptized in water in repentance from sin. When they heard about the baptism of the Holy Spirit, they requested immediately to be baptized in the name of Jesus. That is when Paul laid his hands on them. Guess what happened next. The Holy Spirit came upon them, and they spoke in other tongues and prophesied.

This is why you need to read the Bible for yourself. You cannot just listen to what people are saying from the pulpit or on YouTube. You cannot let them take sections out of the Bible. They cannot just preach grace. They cannot just preach salvation. They cannot just preach hell. They cannot just preach prophecy. You need to hear Genesis to Revelation. You need to hear every page that is in Scripture. You need to know everything that God has said with nothing left out.

If you are a pastor, do not leave anything out. Tell them what the Bible says. They need to know it.

The Power to Speak in Tongues

Let me give you a simple illustration. Imagine this. Before you were saved, you were an empty glass that was supposed to hold something. You were a container to be filled by God, but you had nothing in you, nothing to give, so you lived an empty life. On the day of your salvation, the Holy Spirit filled you. You were filled, but the process was not finished. That process is all you get in some churches because they do not teach you to finish the process that is outlined in Scripture.

But then you let me lay hands on you to baptize you in the Holy Spirit. God takes your full glass that is filled with the Spirit, and He baptizes you. This creates an extension of God's power in your life.

All 27 books in the New Testament were written by Spirit-filled, tongue-talking believers. Everything you read in the New Testament. Let's look at the authors of these books quickly.

Matthew was an apostle baptized at Pentecost.

Mark was led by the Lord and by Peter (theologians say). Paul and Barnabas would take him on missionary journeys.

Luke was a close associate and traveling companion to Paul. He was baptized in the Holy Spirit.

John was an apostle baptized at Pentecost.

Luke wrote the book of Acts. You could not write the book of Acts without having the Holy Spirit!

Paul wrote Romans.

Paul wrote 1st and 2nd Corinthians. He says, "I speak in tongues more than any of you" (1 Corinthians 14:18).

Galatians, Paul said he was baptized in the Holy Spirit.

Ephesians, Paul said he spoke in tongues.

Paul wrote Philippians.

Colossians, Paul said he was filled with the Spirit.

Paul wrote 1st and 2nd Thessalonians.

Paul wrote 1st and 2nd Timothy.

Paul wrote Titus.

Paul wrote Philemon.

It is generally believed that Paul wrote Hebrews.

James, the half-brother of Jesus, was baptized at Pentecost.

First and 2nd Peter were written by Peter, an apostle baptized at Pentecost.

Jude was a half-brother of Jesus, and he was baptized at Pentecost.

Revelation was written by John the Beloved, who was baptized at Pentecost.

There is not one book in the New Testament that was not written by a Holy Spirit–filled author. They all spoke in tongues. Every time you read a book or verse in the New Testament, you are taking the word of someone who spoke in tongues. People who speak out against the Holy Spirit but still use New Testament Scripture are using the words of someone who spoke in tongues. This is so important to understand.

THERE IS NOT ONE BOOK IN THE NEW TESTAMENT THAT WAS NOT WRITTEN BY A HOLY SPIRIT– FILLED AUTHOR.

I want you to have a power revival. I want you to experience and be equipped by the power of the Holy Spirit in your life. I have listed below just a few reasons why you need the Holy Spirit. Please do not just read them quickly and move on. Make it a point to search up the references and see for yourself. I do not want you to take my word for it.

The Spirit of the Lord will fight for you—Isaiah 59:19.

The Spirit will give you rest—Isaiah 63:14.

The Spirit will be your breath—Job 27:3.

The Spirit will fellowship with you—2 Corinthians 13:14.

The Spirit will help you preach—1 Peter 1:12.

The Spirit will help you worship—Philippians 3:3.

The Spirit will help you wait on the Lord—Galatians 5:5.

The Spirit will anoint you—1 John 2:20.

The Spirit will help you love the Lord—Romans 5:5.

The Spirit will guide you—John 16:13.

The Spirit will teach you—1 John 2:27.

The Spirit will give you power—Acts 1:8.

The Spirit will come for you—John 14:16.

The Spirit will reveal—1 Corinthians 2:10.

The Spirit will appoint—Acts 20:28.

The Spirit will command—Acts 16:18.

The Spirit will testify—John 15:26.

The Spirit will intercede—Romans 8:27.

The Spirit will witness—Galatians 4:6.

The Spirit will speak—Acts 2:4.

The Spirit will give you boldness—Acts 4:13.

A Holy Spirit Change

My wife, my beautiful wife, was a believer, but she was not filled with the Spirit when she went to college. Like many young people, she did not get along with her mom. And she would tell you that she did not like her mom. On a Sunday night she got baptized in the Holy Spirit.

Other than her speaking in tongues, she did not think much had changed. But the next day, she noticed immediately that there were differences. She woke up loving her mom, which was a miracle. It just changed. And when she read the Bible, she understood it. The Spirit was teaching her and revealing the Word to her. As if that was not enough, she realized she wanted to witness to everyone. The Holy Spirit changed my wife!

The Holy Spirit has the ability to realign you to where you need to be with God. All Scripture says that you have a choice. You can still live the ho-hum life if you want, but if you choose to do that, you are going to be missing out on the power you need to live abundantly and effectively for God.

Do you know when you do not need the infilling of the Holy Spirit? If in about thirty seconds you are going to die.

Only then will you not need it because you are going to heaven. You do not need the Holy Spirit there. But if you are going to live any length of time on this earth, you need the Holy Spirit to survive. You need the Holy Spirit to help you live holy, to help you make needed changes and to help you fulfill God's call upon your life.

If you are not yet filled with the Spirit, what are you afraid of? Are you scared of the third Person of the Godhead, of the Trinity? I believe that Jesus would say to you, "I want you to have it as My gift to you. He is going to help you live life to the fullest. He is going to reinforce you. He is going to give you spiritual steroids for your spiritual muscles so that you can better fight the enemy. He is going to help you stay righteous and pure. He is going to help you hold on to your joy in the midst of the storm. The Holy Spirit is going to be your peace. He is going to bubble up inside you."

You must cultivate a hunger for the Holy Spirit just as you were hungry for God when you got saved. You came to an altar saying, "I've got a wrecked life here. I haven't done much for You, God. I can't contribute anything. I'm not offering You a whole lot, but what I have, I give You. I give You all of me."

How much did you really offer God when you offered your life? You did not give Him much. I didn't give Him much. He gave me everything because I was desperate. I came humbly, and I wanted it.

Why does God not let everyone speak in tongues? It is not like salvation. Salvation is for everyone. You have to want the Holy Spirit. You have to seek Him. You have to run toward Him. You have to hunger and thirst. You have to knock. You have to ask.

If you do not want the Holy Spirit, fine. You do not have to have it. Struggle the rest of your life. That is fine. If that is what you want to do, that is your choice. But if you are tired of living an average life, tired of living in mediocrity, and you want something greater like revival, you can receive the Holy Spirit!

If you desire the Holy Spirit today, pray this with me.

God, I desire Your Holy Spirit. I desire the gift You promised to give me. I am seeking You out. I am going to get into the Word and believe that You will reward me as I seek Your will for my life. I am knocking on Your door, God. I want what You have for me, and I will pursue it until I receive it. Thank You for Your great gift. Thank You for giving the gift of the Holy Spirit to me. In Jesus' name, Amen.

11 | The Part You Play in Revival

As a global Church, I think that we have lost our conscience. We have lost our common sense. The Bible says that when a nation has the symptoms of sin that I see, it is as if the whole head is sick, and we have putrefying sores as a nation (see Isaiah 1:4–7).

I want all believers to be a Church that reaches out to people. You know as well as I do that there are people in your family, your friends and at your workplace who are away from God. They are loved ones. We all have them. And they are away from God. We want to see them saved, right? They have no hope other than Jesus and no one to tell them other than us. For this reason, we should get out into the world and share the Gospel.

The light that we have is not only to be on display in a church service. Our excitement and shouting only do so much in the building. We need to do that outside. We have got to do it outside in our communities. That is why I put signs on our church doors that read, "You're entering the harvest field." I want our people to be reminded of their mission as they leave our building. We go out to harvest. Not much harvesting goes on at our campus. The church sanctuary is basically a training ground. It is where we come together as a team, the coach talks to us, he calls the plays and then we go out and do them.

I want to talk to you about a revival that I found in the New Testament. It is within the story of the raising of Lazarus from the dead.

> When all the people heard of Jesus' arrival, they flocked to see him and also to see Lazarus, the man Jesus had raised from the dead. Then the leading priests decided to kill Lazarus, too, for it was because of him that many of the people had deserted them and believed in Jesus.
>
> John 12:9–11

We read that the people not only came to see Jesus, but they wanted to see Lazarus, too. Lazarus was Jesus' big-ticket performance because he had been raised from the dead. This was such a big deal that the leading priests decided to kill Lazarus along with Jesus. Why? Lazarus was His number-one testimony, the key proof that He was the Messiah.

The Bible tells us that it was because of Lazarus that many of the people deserted their religious ways and chose to believe in Jesus. People were astonished that Lazarus had been raised from the dead. They knew that there must be something to the power of Jesus if death was no obstacle to Him.

I can just imagine the priests saying, "Lazarus died once, but he is going to have to die again!" The miracle was just that big. They thought something had to be done to discourage the people from following Jesus.

Lazarus, who was just a normal man, became a trophy of what God had done. It was something absolutely unbelievable. And this news spread. Remember that this is before they had Facebook, Twitter, Instagram or YouTube—they did not have any of those. The news of Lazarus spread by word of mouth throughout the entire city.

It is amazing what word of mouth can do when we get out there and speak about something important. All of a sudden, somebody else who heard what we said runs across the same person, the same waiter or waitress, the same doctor or nurse, and they say the same thing. It is amazing how the message doubles and triples when we are all saying the same thing.

The day after Jesus raised Lazarus, He traveled to Jerusalem, and news of His journey swept through the city. People were talking. If word of mouth was that effective back then, why cannot we get the news spreading throughout our cities about the miracle-working power of Jesus today?

Jesus borrowed a young donkey and rode it into Jerusalem. This fulfilled the prophecy that said, "Shout in triumph, O people of Jerusalem! Look, your king is coming to you. He is righteous and victorious, yet he is humble, riding on a donkey—riding on a donkey's colt" (Zechariah 9:9). His disciples did not understand at the time that this was a fulfillment of prophecy. They were not learned people. This bunch of fishermen did not have Bibles. But after Jesus entered into His glory, they remembered what had happened and realized that these things had been written about Him in the Old Testament, proving that He was their Messiah.

It was Passover, and as Jesus entered the city, visitors took palm branches and went down the road to meet Him. They shouted, "Praise God! Blessings on the one who comes in the name of the Lord! Hail to the King of Israel!" (John 12:13). Many in this crowd had seen Jesus call Lazarus out from the tomb. They were eyewitnesses to the fact that Jesus had raised him from the dead, and they began to tell others about it.

That was the reason Lazarus was raised. This miraculous sign drew the crowds and gave Jesus an audience with the people. "Then the Pharisees said to each other, 'There's nothing we can do. Look, everyone has gone after him!'" (verse 19).

You can have a Lazarus Revival. I have six points that I want to give you. We will cover three points in this chapter:

1. The world is sin-sick.
2. We have a responsibility to the world.
3. Only the second opinion of Jesus counts.

Then, in the next chapter, we will cover the final three points:

1. We must collectively lift Jesus up.
2. We must feel the compassion that Jesus feels for people.
3. We must play a part in the miracle Jesus wants to bring about.

I believe this is one of the most important messages that I have been given to share, and I want to take my time with it. I want you to really understand the power of a Lazarus Revival for your life.

What Drew the People

There was no other time in Jesus' life when He was adored and honored like a monarch than when He came into Jerusalem. The people waved palm branches, shouted and sang out in tremendous joy at His arrival. At no other time in Jesus' life was He celebrated or esteemed to that level. This is why I believe that if we desire to have Jesus in our city, if we want the deliverer to arrive, if we are going to have the Lamb of God who takes away the sin of the world come to town, we are going to have to recognize an element in this story that is often overlooked.

The people did not flock to Jerusalem because they believed that Jesus was the Messiah or that He was on a mission from God. They were not there because they recognized Him as the fulfillment of Old Testament Scripture. They were in the streets because they had either seen or heard about a miracle that had happened in the little village of Bethany. This miracle, in which this man who had been dead for four days, came walking out of his grave.

I believe if we are going to see King Jesus riding into our lives and into our cities, we first need a Lazarus Revival. I am not talking about one man being raised from the dead, although that would do it. I am not necessarily saying that is what we need. I am talking about one great crusade. This principle comes from the Lazarus miracle, and it is so obvious we cannot walk around it any longer. This is what I want to give you. Are you ready for it?

If My People

Let's look at John 11. A man named Lazarus was sick. He lived in Bethany with his sisters, Mary and Martha. This is the Mary who later poured the expensive perfume on the Lord's feet and wiped them with her hair (see Luke 7:36–50). Lazarus was sick, so his two sisters sent a message to Jesus telling Him about it. "Lord, your dear friend is very sick" (verse 3).

Similarly, there was a time when the nation of Israel was also very sick. Through His prophets, God called them to change. He called them through the judges who were appointed over Israel, and He called them through divine intervention. But the people of Israel would not recognize their sickness. So instead of going into the land of promise and plenty, what happened? They wandered in the wilderness where many of them died before receiving their promises.

The book of Revelation includes a letter from God to the church in Ephesus (see Revelation 2:1–7). God says to that church,

> "I know all the things you do. I have seen your hard work and your patient endurance. I know you don't tolerate evil people. . . . You have patiently suffered for me without quitting. But I have this complaint against you. You don't love me or each other as you did at first!"
>
> Revelation 2:2–4

Ask yourself this question: Do I love Jesus now as much as I did when I first started loving Him?

God continues, "If you don't repent, I will come and remove your lampstand [or your light and influence] from its place among the churches" (verse 5).

There is another church, the one in Sardis, that also received a warning (see Revelation 3:1–6). God says in this letter, "I know all the things you do, and that you have a reputation for being alive—but you are dead. Wake up! Strengthen what little remains, for even what is left is almost dead" (verses 1–2). Wow! This is speaking to some of the churches in the world today.

God is saying, "I find that your actions do not meet My requirements. Go back to what you heard and believed at first. Repent, return to Me again and hold to My requirements firmly. If you do not wake up, I will come to you suddenly and as unexpectedly as a thief."

We also read a message to the church in Laodicea (see Revelation 3:14–22). That message is, "I know all the things you do, that you are neither hot nor cold. I wish that you were one or the other! But since you are like lukewarm water, neither hot nor cold, I will spit you out of my mouth!" (verses 15–16).

You say, "Well, I have some hot moments," but you have been ice cold in other areas. That makes you lukewarm. It is time to decide what you are going to do. Make your choice. Quit floating in the middle. Decide where you want to be. This is a strong word from Jehovah God.

These words were not just for the Church two thousand years ago. They are for the Church today. They are for us as individuals today. Jesus is looking for His bride to be committed. Unfortunately, His bride is sick and cannot make a commitment and stick with it. There is a sickness of hypocrisy in the Church today. But we still have time to recognize we are a sick Church, a sick society in general, and that without the intervention of God, we are headed for certain death and eternal separation.

I do not know how Americans can think that they are doing well or that there is no sickness in their land. There is a grave sickness upon them. There is a grave sickness upon the world! This disease of sin has not just infected America; it is everywhere. We need to be honest enough with ourselves to be gripped with this burden of fact and the knowledge that if we do not have a divine intervention, there is going to be no hope at all. We have to be sober and realize this before we can have a Lazarus Revival.

Here are some of the things that have been going on in America and other nations:

A woman whose parents denied taking her to Outback Steakhouse attacks her parents and threatens to kill them.[1]

A twelve-year-old boy shoots his mom eight times and kills her because she asked him to do his chores.[2]

A fourteen-year-old boy shoots his mom while she was sleeping because he could not hang out with his friends.[3]

A six-year-old boy shoots his classmate the day after they had a playground quarrel.[4]

A fifteen-year-old girl shoots her dad with a hunting bow because he took away her cell phone.[5]

An eleven-year-old boy shoots his dad because he did not buy him a gaming console.[6]

We have to recognize that we live in a sick society. I think sometimes we want to push the truth of that away. We want to deny or ignore the fact that there is sin-sickness all around us. But we are in a sick society. You can tell it is a sick society when we are more concerned about harming an eagle's egg than we are about killing an unborn child. We have a sickness.

Sickness is when we have multiple millions of dollars spent to rehabilitate alcoholics while we sponsor every teenage sporting event with beer commercials.

Sickness is when we tell our youth in public schools that pornography is healthy.

Sickness is when Planned Parenthood can boldly recommend sex toys to our students while the Bible is forbidden on our campuses.

Sickness is when it is legal to pass out condoms to teenagers for safe sex instead of teaching our kids that the best way not to contract a sexually transmitted disease is to stay a virgin.

Sickness is when freedom of speech is demanded for the lesbian, the homosexual, the pornographer, the atheist and the haters of Christianity, but it is denied a few kids on campus who want to pray in a public classroom.

Sickness is when our daughters cannot drive on a city street at night, and our children cannot walk safely in our own neighborhoods.

Sickness is when we need security guards and X-ray machines to enter our public schools.

Sickness is when we are more concerned with mass shootings than we are about stopping the behavior that is causing it.

Sickness is when we in the Church are more concerned with prestige, power and success than we are about souls.

Sickness is when we are more focused on real estate than righteousness, and when we are more focused on progress than we are on prayer, reputation or repentance.

This world is so sick that our children are cyberbullying themselves.[7] It is true. Teens who spend five hours or more on the cell phone are 70 percent more likely to have suicidal thoughts.[8] They are filling their minds with negative things all day long. And now this digital self-harm has shown up.

We need to hear 2 Chronicles 7:14 again. "If my people who are called by my name will humble themselves and pray and seek my face and turn from their wicked ways, I will hear from heaven and will forgive their sins and restore their land." Those called out are not the Church, and they are not the city. God says, "I'm looking for My people. Who are My people who will stand in the gap for their nation? Who will humble themselves, pray and seek Me?"

It is up to us. It is not the Democrats. It is not the Republicans. It is not the president. It is not Congress. It is not the Senate. If you live outside the United States, it is not your government, either. If you are waiting for someone to turn things around, look in the mirror. There is not anybody who can do it except for you and me. We are His people. We have to get serious.

IF YOU ARE WAITING FOR SOMEONE TO TURN THINGS AROUND, LOOK IN THE MIRROR.

Returning to our passage about Lazarus, word came from Mary and Martha saying, "Jesus, the one you love is gravely sick." Jesus loves this world, and this world is sick.

God did not just love the world in Bible times but then lose that love today. No, He still loves the world. He still loves the people in the world. Make no mistake about it. Jesus loves the prostitute who walks the streets. Jesus loves the drug addict with the needle hanging out of his arm. Jesus loves the abortionist who has ripped children from the wombs of their mothers. Jesus loves the man who has walked out on his family and left his kids crying at home. Jesus even loves the one who is on death row for murder. Jesus loves the biggest hypocrite there is, and He loves you and me because this is who Jesus is.

With all the love He has for us, we have got to understand that there is no one else God is going to look to in terms of changing this world. He says, "It is going to be My people." Realize this responsibility. If you are sitting and waiting for someone to come in and help the situation, you will be waiting forever. It rests on you to step in for your family, for your church and for your town or city. You cannot deal with everything, but you can deal with where God places you. Oh God, use us!

A Second Opinion

For us to have a Lazarus Revival, Jesus must receive all the glory. When Jesus heard about Lazarus's sickness, He said, "Lazarus's sickness will not end in death. No, it happened for the glory of God so that the Son of God will receive glory from this" (John 11:4). It happened for God's glory. It will not end in death.

If we are going to have a Lazarus Revival to bring Jesus victoriously into our city as King, Deliverer and Savior, we need to get a second opinion. It is always good to get a second opinion, because, as you see, the first opinion is usually depressing. Yeah, I just said it.

The first opinion was that they were to go to hospice. The first opinion was that you are going to die. The first opinion was that it is all over. But then there was a second opinion.

A Heart on Fire

The second opinion is the only one that really matters because that is the opinion of the Master. We need to have the opinion of the One who is able to do exceedingly and abundantly above all that you ask or think (see Ephesians 3:20). We need the opinion of the One who knows the end from the beginning. We can listen to the prognosis of man, or we can listen to the prognosis of God. Which will you choose?

The economists want to say that we are going to have an economic collapse. But the second opinion says, "I have never seen the godly abandoned or their children begging for bread" (Psalm 37:25).

Scientists and politicians say global warming will kill us all. But I have a second opinion that says, "No, it is a global *warning*. It is what it is."

Banks and savings and loan companies are closing their doors. But the second opinion says, "I own the cattle on a thousand hills" (Psalm 50:10).

Military experts say it is going to end in war. But the second opinion says, "No, it is going to end with a trumpet."

The doctor says it is incurable and there is no hope. But the second opinion says, "By his wounds you are healed" (1 Peter 2:24).

The devil says he is going to destroy you. He is going to ruin you. He is going to win. But the second opinion says, "Devil, you are going to lose, you are going to run and you are going to tremble."

If you are overwhelmed by anything in your life right now, you need a second opinion. Praise God, there is an alternative to the gloom. I praise God for all the people who are talking on television. I have Scripture passages that totally counter what they are saying. I have Scripture passages that build me up.

170

They are not reading what I am reading. They do not know the God that I know. They do not have the hope that I have. I would be hopeless if I did not know God or if I did not know the Bible. I would be just like them. But thank God, I have Him. I have a church community. I have people who build me up so that I can keep praising God and get my strength back.

See, when you walk in the presence of God, there is fullness of joy. I do not have that in the world. In Him, I have fullness of joy. I have peace in the midst of storms. Trust me, I need a pep talk every day, but I have a Word that is sharper than any two-edged sword that will tell me what I need to hear. Amen!

When Jesus Delays

We see in our Bible passage that Jesus loved Martha. He loved Mary. He would spend nights with Lazarus when He was traveling nearby. He had a room at their house. They were good friends. They served Him, took care of Him and let Him rest. And although Jesus loved them (as He loves you), He stayed where He was for the next two days even after He heard about Lazarus's death. Does that make any sense to you? "I love you so much that I am not coming."

How many times have we asked God to come into the midst of a situation we are facing but His answer was not what we expected? We pray, "God, I keep hearing about all Your great love, but where are You now? I don't feel the love right now when I need it the most."

Have you ever gotten to the place where you wondered where God was in your difficult time? "God, if You are everywhere, You are hiding, because I don't know where You went. I don't know where You are. I can't feel You."

We have a wrong understanding about something. God comes, but He does not always come right away. You may have a need, and God says, "I'm not coming." It does not seem logical that Jesus would say this to His close friends—especially when the friend He loved was deathly ill. Lazarus was so sick he that died, but even in this most desperate of times, Jesus stayed two more days. What would that be like?

If my wife, Deborah, called me and said, "Glen, I am not feeling well. I am in a hospital. I don't know if I'm going to make it through the night," what kind of a husband would I be if I responded, "Okay. I will see you in a couple days"? I will have you know that she would live long enough to kill me!

She would say, "Get me out of this bed. I will come back and die later. But let me go get him first!" I am just trying to put in perspective how odd Jesus' response was to Mary and Martha. You receive a message that someone you love is in need, but you decide not to come. That is strange! Even stranger is that He was the only One who had the ability to do the miraculous. They did not know anyone else who could do that. And He did not drop everything and run to them. Just think about that.

Trust God's Timing

To have a Lazarus Revival, you have to trust God's timing. You have to trust Him. Let me say this, the worst conclusion you can arrive at is that God is not going to intervene in your situation because He has not thus far.

See, God has a timing that is designed so that miracles and occurrences in our life will bring Him the greatest glory. How many times has God used something bad to move you into something good? Think about that. How many times did you think it was hopeless, but all God wanted was to build your faith and trust in Him?

As we mature as believers, we find out that storms are inevitable. Everybody experiences them. All a storm does is reveal who you are. It reveals if you are going to have faith or if you are going to give up. It reveals whether you are going to whine and complain or you are going to pray and hold on to God's promises.

What are you going to do in the midst of your storm? Every time something happens to you, are you ready to bail on God? The devil will make sure that there is something to push you out of your comfy place, so you might as well anticipate that you are going to go through hard things.

You have to get to the point that regardless of the circumstances—whether sun or storm, whatever the weather, whatever is going on in your life—you are at ease and can handle it. You are going to keep walking, and you are not going to fall down. You are going to keep moving forward, and you are not going to stop. You are going to buck up and be a man or woman of God because God says it is time for you to grow up.

Many believers I know have gotten angry when God did not show up on their timetable. They began to criticize Him and call Him a bunch of names, which always brings God closer to you, right? Do you think it would ever work to get mad at God and huff and puff, fold your arms and dish out ultimatums? I do not really think God would respond like, "Oh, man! Hey, Gabriel, do you hear what he is calling Me? I am going to have to help him out because he just chewed Me out. I have to go now!" Where do we see in Scripture that if you chew God out, He will show up? Nowhere? Well then, stop it! That is immature and a sign of a lack of trust and respect.

You are a grown-up. By now, you should be able to handle the devil and tell him where he needs to go. You should be able to keep walking with God.

You wonder why God is not using you. You wonder why you are not at another level by now or why you have not had breakthrough. Could it be that you are harboring spiritual immaturity? Could it be that you are not willing to buck up and do what God expects you to do? What will it take for you to mature to the place where you can say, "Let the storm come into my life. It doesn't matter! Whether it storms or not, it is not going to change where I stand. I am not going to fold. I am not going to fall. God is my rock. I am going to keep standing."

What if what you are going through is not for your benefit but for the glory of God to be seen through you so that other people will believe? Maybe you need to quit whining about what this is going to do for you because it may not do anything for you. It might just be a testimony for somebody outside the Body of Christ who does not believe the show.

The world quits when things get tough, but you and I do not quit because we have God. That speaks to the world. Have you ever had somebody ask you, "How could you go through all that and not lose your mind? How could you go through that without taking pills or being depressed?" When you are a true believer, you can say, "Because I have God in me, and He is the peace that passes all understanding."

God's timing is different from your timing. He does not wear a watch. He *is* time. Time to Him is nothing that you could possibly understand. If it is not going to bring Him glory in this moment, He is going to wait. "Well, yeah, but I need it now." You say you want a good testimony, and He is trying to give you one. But you will not be patient. The worst conclusion you could ever arrive at is that God is not going to intervene because He has not done so yet. It does not mean that at all.

God wants you to wake up. We live in a sick society, and we have been called by God to be healers by standing in the gap in humility, in prayer and in seeking His face. We must recognize that if *we* do not do something, nothing is going to change. The reason we are not experiencing revival is because the Church has good people who are not doing anything. We only have a few people who are committed to making an impact for the Kingdom.

Could we live and die without our friends knowing what we believe and why? Is there a possibility that you could die but your friends could never have known that you were a Christian? Will they find that out at your funeral? Will they wonder why you never really said anything about it? They would likely think more of you if you said something to them. They would at least know that you cared enough to be honest.

Recognize we are in a sick society. It seems as if when you are watching CNN or Fox news, or whatever news you watch, there is always something tragic and something horrible going on. It never used to be that way, but now it is common. The younger generations expect it. It is common to them. But I am telling you, this is wrong. Our society is crazy. We have lost our minds. We need God. We need God to come back. We need a second opinion on things.

When the devil tells you that you are worthless, when he tells you that you are no good, when he tells you that you will never amount to anything, when he tells you that your past is going to dictate your future, you need to talk to the One who has a second opinion for your life. God has another opinion about you. He thinks more of you than what you think of yourself at times.

175

I hope you take away from this chapter that you need to trust God's timing on things. Sometimes you will have to wait longer than you want, but there is a reason for the wait. Trust Him. You might be thinking, "I waited, and I don't know where He is. Why isn't He coming? Doesn't He love me? If He does, He should come right now." I am telling you that God has something bigger planned than you can imagine, and when it does come to pass, you will understand the reason for the wait.

If you are reading this and think that you need a Lazarus Revival in your life, you need a change and you need a resurrection, let me pray for you.

Lord Jesus, touch my friend today. He or she needs a life change. He needs his sins forgiven. She needs hope, peace, a sound mind and a Savior. Lord, I ask You to take what he or she has and make something great out of it. There is potential in my reader that needs to come out, but first he or she has to get the enemy and sin out of the way. So I ask You, Lord, to take the past, bury it, forgive him or her and help the reader get excited about his or her future in You. It starts right now. In Jesus' name, Amen.

12 | How to Have
a Lazarus Revival

A group of Jews were traveling from town to town casting out evil spirits (see Acts 19). They were the seven sons of Sceva, the leading priest at the time. Basically, they were vagabonds or gypsies who traveled around performing exorcisms. That is how they made money. They tried to use the name of the Lord Jesus in their incantations, saying, "I command you in the name of Jesus, whom Paul preaches, to come out!" (verse 13). The only problem was, they were not believers. They were simply borrowing a powerful name and hoping it would work for them. I hope you know you are not able to move anything with a borrowed anointing. It will not work.

One time when they tried to perform an exorcism, the evil spirit replied, "I know Jesus, and I know Paul, but who are you?" (verse 15). The devil knows the Lord, but who are you? Then the man with the evil spirit leapt on them and overpowered the seven sons. He attacked with such violence that they fled from the house naked and battered. Who knew there would be so many streakers in the New Testament!

The devil knows Jesus. He knows Jesus better than most believers do. He knows His power, and he respects that power more than we often do. He respects what comes out of the mouth of Jesus. This is why you cannot use the name of Jesus when you do not know Him, when you are not in right relationship with Him. It will not work. It will only reveal your spiritual condition.

The seven sons of Sceva were scared. They were scared like a long-tailed cat in a rocking chair factory. They were as scared as a hog at a barbecue.

See, when you are fighting the devil and he attacks your life, a false faith will expose your weakness and lack of spiritual authority. You cannot borrow my armor. You cannot borrow the anointing that God has placed in me. If you are wondering why your financial miracle has not come or why you are not married yet, you have really got to buckle down and trust God's timing.

God leads, Satan pushes. One more time: God leads, Satan pushes. When you feel pushed, you feel as if you have to make something work. That is the devil pushing you. Do not give in to that. Let God work it out for you. Just follow Him. He is ready and willing to orchestrate your whole life if you will just let Him. You do not have to do anything on your own.

The Sleep of Death

In the previous chapter, we began reading the story of Lazarus being raised from the dead. We are going to pick it back up. I strongly suggest you get your Bible and read this section for yourself.

Jesus said to His disciples, "'Let's go back to Judea.' But his disciples objected. 'Rabbi,' they said, 'only a few days ago the people in Judea were trying to stone you'" (John 11:8). Jesus was not concerned with the threats. He told them, "There are twelve hours of daylight every day. During the day people can walk safely. They can see because they have the light of this world. But at night there is danger of stumbling because they have no light" (verses 9–10). He was telling them there was no need to fear. He was with them, and He is the light of the world.

I want you to catch this. Jesus was asking His disciples, "Do you think that I'm going to go into darkness and fall into a trap? Do you understand who I am? I am light. I can't go into darkness because darkness runs from Me. As long as you have light, as long as you have Me, you're going to be okay." Darkness cannot hurt us when we have Jesus.

Jesus then proceeded to tell His disciples that Lazarus had fallen asleep, and His reason for wanting to go now was to wake him up. If I had been there, I think I would have asked, "Isn't falling asleep a good thing? Isn't rest good? Won't he get better if he can get some rest? Why would You want to wake him? If it's that important, can't Mary or Martha do it?"

The disciples had similar thoughts. They said, "If he is sleeping, he will soon get better" (verse 12). Jesus, knowing that they were not catching what He was saying, broke it down for them. "Lazarus is dead. And for your sakes, I'm glad I wasn't there, for now you will really believe" (verses 14–15).

All of this took place not long before He rode into Jerusalem on the colt. The following Friday, they threw Him into jail and crucified Him. We are not far away from that story. All of these events happened at the end of Jesus' life.

Jesus arrived four days after Lazarus had died (because healing a dead man is more marvelous than healing a sick man). If you have ever wondered if sarcasm is in the Bible, here is the most sarcastic statement you could ever read. Here is our buddy Thomas, doubting, foot-shaped mouth Thomas, saying to his fellow disciples, "Let's go, too—and die with Jesus" (verse 16). Hmm. That translates in my ears to, "Hey, if He wants to go back there and get stoned, we might as well die with Him." Not exactly the most encouraging disciple in the group.

Too Late for a Miracle

The town of Bethany was only a few miles away, so it would only take a couple of hours to walk if you were not in a hurry. Many others had already come a long distance to console Mary and Martha. For that to be mentioned in the Bible, you know they were influential people. People knew Mary, Martha and Lazarus. They were a prominent family. Yet Jesus, their close family friend, arrived from a short distance four days late.

When Martha received word that Jesus was coming, she went to meet Him. Mary stayed at the house. Martha said to Jesus, "Lord, if only you had been here, my brother would not have died" (verse 21). She was not upset. She was just saying what you and I would have said if something like this had happened to us. "Jesus, it's too late now for a miracle. Where were You when we needed You? If You would have answered, we would not be in this situation right now." But even in her matter-of-factness, she said, "But even now I know that God will give you whatever you ask" (verse 22).

Can you believe that? Can you accept that it does not matter how bad it looks? God is able to speak a word and change it. If you cannot believe that, then do not expect a miracle.

Jesus told Martha, "Your brother will rise again" (verse 23). That right there is such a statement of confidence, don't you think? "My word is that your brother is going to rise again." He did not say, "You know what? I am going to give it My best shot. Let's see what happens. I am going to pray, and sometimes what I pray for happens. Sometimes it does not. We will just see what happens today. Who knows what God is feeling. I will just give it a shot." No, no. He was very confident.

"Your brother will rise again." Martha did not quite get it. She said, "Yeah, I know. He is going to rise again when everybody else rises in the last days," meaning when everybody is raptured and goes to heaven. She was not thinking about an immediate healing. In her mind, it was too late. He was gone.

Jesus told her, "I am the resurrection and the life" (verse 25). He was reminding her, "I am your Healer. I am your Savior. I am your Hope. I am your Peace. I Am." Whatever you need, Jesus is it to you. You see, He is the resurrection and the life, and anyone who believes in Him will live even after dying. He said, "Martha, do you believe this?" And now I am asking you: What do you believe?

Do you believe without any reservation or restriction that Jesus is the resurrection and the life? If you believe in Him, you will live. You have got to believe that whatever is dead in your life can still be resurrected by God. He can take what is dead, what is buried and what is totally over and He can breathe life into it. He can speak a word unto it, and it can come alive.

When Revival Happens

Revival happens when we collectively, jointly, in every section of our city, lift Jesus up. You know what? It is time to quit hating people because they have a different opinion. Come on! It is as though you bought a white car and I bought a red car, so I do not like you. I mean, we have got to stop this. It is time to quit discussing how terrible our society is. We know it is bad, but to keep discussing it is not healing anything. We need to stop discussing the dreaded disease of compromise and carnality that has walked into our homes. We have got to quit discussing all of these problems that we have. No matter how complex the problem is, it is not over. The Bible says it is not over as long as there is someone named Healer, Hope and Prince of Peace.

It is not that He can heal. He is your Healer. It is not that He can supply your needs. He is the Supplier of your needs. Jesus is the same yesterday, today and forever. Do not look to the left. Do not look to the right. Do not read the morning newspaper. Do not look at the evening news. "Look to Me," God says, "because I Am that I Am. There is nobody else." Yes, Lord!

Martha never stopped believing in Jesus. She said, "I've never stopped believing who You are. You're the One who came into the world from God. I know this." Then she returned to Mary and called her aside from the mourners so that they would not see Jesus. Then Mary went to Him immediately. When the people in the house consoling Mary saw her leave so hastily, they assumed she was going to Lazarus's grave to weep, so they followed her there. Mary arrived at the tomb, saw Jesus and fell at His feet saying, "Lord, if only you had been here" (verse 32).

I think we have all said something similar to what Mary said. If Jesus had been there, He would have had the ability to do this or take care of that situation. But watch this: "When Jesus saw her weeping and saw the other people wailing with her, a deep anger welled up within him, and he was deeply troubled" (verse 33). He got angry at the Pharisees earlier in His ministry. He got angry at the money changers in the temple. And He got angry when He saw Mary weeping. Do you know what He was angry about? Death and the grave.

Death took someone He loved. That is the moment I believe He decided, "Okay, I was just going to deal with hell and get that key, but now I think I am going to get the keys of death and the grave as well. I am going to get all three keys, and the devil will never own death again. My people will never know death and the grave if they follow Me." Never will they know death and grave again. That is just powerful.

The Compassion of Jesus

Next we read, "Then Jesus wept" (verse 35). He wept. He had feelings. He cared. He loved. To have a Lazarus Revival, we must feel the compassion that Jesus feels for people. Do you understand? We cannot have compassion for people if we are still hurting over things. If you remain wounded, you are not dealing with your issues. You cannot help anybody with their pain because poor, pitiful you has had such a horrible life. It is as if you keep living specific days of your life over and over again, focusing on your wounds and not on the goodness of God in your life.

> **WE MUST FEEL THE COMPASSION THAT JESUS FEELS FOR PEOPLE.**

Compassion is the ability to alleviate, remove or reduce the suffering of another. That is what believers do. You are healed to heal others. God brings you out so that you can help someone else get out. Have compassion. Go out and feed people. Take care of families and kids. Work with a mobile dental clinic or a mobile medical clinic. Do free mechanic work for widows and single parents. Take a stand against human trafficking. Support missions and spread the Gospel to the world. Provide clean drinking water to the indigent. Take care of people. It is not all about you. It is not all about me. It is not all about how we feel. There is always somebody who is worse off than you.

A Lazarus Revival is when we stand at the tomb of our city and weep for it. We see the hurt, pain and suffering. God, help us not to lose our compassion for the lost and those in need.

I just want to point out that Jesus did not weep over a Church. He wept over a city (see Luke 19:41). Scripture says He wept and cried over a city. He cried because He felt the pain, because He suffered with and was able to feel the pain of what the people were going through. He was moved in His inward parts. That is what the word *compassion* means.

Remove the Stone

Nobody had the backbone to say what Jesus said when Lazarus was dead and buried. This was the champion of all statements—an unbelievable statement that was delivered with no hesitation: "Roll the stone away." Did He roll the stone away Himself? No. Did He command Lazarus to do it? No.

Jesus does not want to do the miracle by Himself. He could have, but He wanted others to play a part in the miracle. He wants the same for you today. He is inviting you to be part of the miracle that He is about to do because it will change your life. And you know what? It takes a lot of faith to trust Him in that moment. I can hear the bystanders now.

"Is He talking to us?"

"Is He serious?"

"He wants us to do what?"

"I think He actually does!"

"Let's have a committee meeting and we'll decide who gets to do it then."

"Do you want to do it, Henry?"

"Not me. My back. I hurt my back. Not able to push. Bobby, what about you?"

"Well, I was going to play in the NFL, but I hurt my ankle in elementary school. I can't do it."

"What about you, Sally? Would you want to go and help? You're kind of a bodybuilder. You pull up pretty strong."

"No, I didn't sleep well last night."

"I don't think I can make it over there." Do you hear? Do you hear them getting together and discussing?

I am sure we have all had thoughts like, *I'm not going to look like a fool going up there and rolling that thing away when a dead man is rotting in there.* You would have had to have been crazy to believe. I am sure the Pharisees who were present thought Jesus had lost His mind. But a bunch of brave people heard what He said, and they followed His direction. I bet they were glad they did! I bet they were glad to have been a part of this miracle.

Why is it so hard for us to hear the Lord order us to do something? In our minds we have a conversation about whether we are going to do it or not. *I don't know if I should get involved.*

Jesus knew that if He did not show that Lazarus was dead, people would not have believed. They would have thought it was a trick of some sort. He made sure even the doubters were right there, participating in the miracle. Jesus asked, "Didn't I tell you that you would see God's glory if you believe?" (John 11:40).

The people rolled the stone aside. Then Jesus looked to heaven and said, "Father, thank you for hearing me. You always hear me, but I said it out loud for the sake of all these people standing here, so that they will believe you sent me" (verses 41–42). He acknowledged that the miracle that was about to happen was not about Him. He was simply doing His Father's business, what His Father told Him to do. He was determined to bring God glory and connect people to Him.

It is our responsibility to remove the stone. It is up to you and me to help people remove the stones from their graves. It is up to you and me to help people come into the Kingdom of God. The bottom line is that the people we deal with do not have the capacity to get themselves up and come to a church, get help, go to a hospital or whatever. They cannot do it. That is why we have to remove the barriers that are restricting them and lead them out.

We are God's instruments of harmony, are we not? And we, as instruments, do His work. We act as conduits for Him to do His work through us.

We are His arms to bring love.

We are His feet to bring food and freedom.

We are His words to bring hope.

We are His soldiers to push back darkness.

We are His hands for the helpless.

We are His smile for the oppressed.

We are His keys for those who are bound.

We are His provision for the vision.

We are His house for the stranger.

We are His altar for the convicted.

We are His help for the divorced.
We are His aid for the homeless.
We are His counsel for the addicted.
We are His safety for the abused.
We are His Church for the prostitute.
We are His Church for the pornographer.
We are His Church for the homosexual.
We are His Church for the atheist.

We are also the Church for rich young rulers, for CEOs, for celebrities, for doctors, for lawyers, for performers, for computer programmers and entrepreneurs. We are His Church for the "thousandaires" and the millionaires.

We, as believers, are to be God-led, people-loving friends of sinners. We should reject no one because we love our city. We love people. We need—and they need—a Lazarus Revival.

Christianity involves other people. You are never so spiritual that you can just sit at home. You may go to heaven, but you are not really going as a Christian. The Bible tells us we are to pray for one another, heal one another and help one another. How can we sit at home and help one another? We cannot do that. We have got to come outside. That is why many churches have life groups. They want their members to get actively involved in each other's lives.

People respond to a demonstration of love, not an explanation of love. You can talk about love all you want, but it is far better to express it. See, for a Lazarus Revival to happen, we need people who are willing to remove the stone. God needs you to remove the stone.

Jesus shouted, "Lazarus, come out!" If He would not have called Lazarus specifically, every grave would have opened up.

Uncle Henry would have been back. They would have seen Grandpa Walter and Aunt Millie come walking out.

The dead man came out by himself. His hands and feet were bound in grave clothes, his face wrapped like a mummy. Jesus told them to unwrap him. It is as if He was saying, "I don't want the people who removed the stone to do this part. They have already been part of the miracle. Give Me some new people. Give Me some people who know how to unwrap somebody."

Lazarus was resurrected. He was alive. But he was walking strangely because of the wrappings. He could not talk because his mouth was wrapped. He could not really see because his eyes were wrapped. He was wrapped like a mummy because he had been dead. But now he was alive! He was resurrected, but he was still bound.

People will get saved and walk out of their situations, but they will still be wrapped in some grave clothes from their past. Maybe their problem is that they have given up. They have said, "I can't get out of this. I'm too bound." They do not understand Lazarus could not get out of his grave clothes, either. That is why Jesus called for others to help.

"Come help him. Come help her. Unwrap the areas of the world—pull it off them—because they can't do it themselves."

In this passage we find three kinds of people:

We have those who are saved and who are living free with no grave clothes.

We have those who are dead in the tomb. They are gone spiritually. They do not even know if they are going to heaven. They are hopeless. They need a resurrection.

And we have those who are trying to come out. They have been resurrected, but they have still got a stench. It is the stench of this world still on them. They are fighting it and doing everything they possibly can, but they are bound. They need help. They need somebody to unwrap them. Their hands are tied, their mouths are shut and their eyes are closed. They need you to set them free.

Will you help rescue them? They may have been abused when they were children. Their fathers or mothers may have beaten them. Maybe they were abandoned, and their remaining parent had to work hard days and late hours to make ends meet. Even though that parent did everything he or she could to help, the children are still bound. They still need help.

It is our job, our calling, to help. Lazarus was not embarrassed that he was wrapped in grave clothes. If he had been embarrassed, he would have waited to come out until people came into the tomb to unwrap him. Then he would have come out. But see, once you get free enough to walk, then it is not too hard to walk another twenty or thirty feet to get your grave clothes pulled off.

Maybe today you are the one in the tomb. You are spiritually dead. Jesus had not called your name, but He is calling it now. Just listen. He is calling it now. Can you imagine Him calling your name?

"Billy, come forth."

"Andrea, come forth."

"Christy, come forth."

"Bobby, come forth."

"Andy, come forth."

He is calling your name, specifically. And if you hear Him, He is the resurrection and the life. Listen, if you do not get this today, I do not know if you are ever going to get anything I say. This is about as clear as your condition gets in Scripture. Seriously, it says that it is your choice. You do what you want to do. All I know is that I will stand before God one day and say, "God, I tried."

God is going to remind you of this moment when you are reading this book. It is your decision to make Christ the Lord of your life. It is your decision to respond to the voice of Jesus when He calls your name.

It is your decision. God does not send people to hell. You send yourself there by your own choice. You cannot blame God for this. Why would God send someone to hell? God does not do that. So if today you recognize that you are dead spiritually—you do not know if you are going to heaven, you are not sure—then you need a resurrection. You need God to call your name. Lazarus heard the call and walked out of his tomb. And I hear God calling you now, so walk out. Come on. It is your moment for a miracle!

Maybe today you have walked out of your tomb. You are saved, but you are still in your grave clothes. You still have a stench in your life. You are crawling instead of walking or running, and you are barely making it. You want to get unwrapped. You are ready to take off the wrappings from this world and get the stench out of your life. You are ready to get free. You are ready to live life again. If that is you, maybe the devil is fighting you more than ever right now because he knows he is about to get a whooping. I want you to know that nothing can hold you back any longer.

Take your right hand and put it on your heart in an act of faith. I want you to know we are in the same fight together. We are not so different. We are in the same fight. I need you. You need me. We need each other in this. Look, I know you are tired. You have been hindered at every turn. You feel incomplete, imperfect and soiled. God wants to remove all of this from you. I am here to help take off your grave clothes. I am the willing instrument Jesus is using to unwrap you from your past.

Jesus wept, and He is weeping now. There is a compassion that went forth when He wept and saw Lazarus, and today, He is with you. The tears are rolling down His cheeks, and He is ready to unwrap your pain and your suffering, your mistakes, your setbacks, your sins, the things you have said, the stuff you have done and even the people who have hurt you so that you can forgive them.

Let's pray together.

Lord Jesus, I humbly stand before You in my grave clothes. I am stuck. I am hindered. I am delayed. I am tired of thinking the same old way, speaking the same old way and believing the same old way. But I am waking up. Today is a wake-up day. I realize there is help. I realize how much You want to help me. So Lord, resurrect the spirit that is dead in me. Resurrect it to life and unwrap these grave clothes, these things in my past, the issues I have dealt with and the sins I have committed. Take the stench that I hate out of my life, and let the fragrance, the sweet fragrance of Christ, pour on me like a perfume of healing. God, I am here because I love You. I did not know I could be free, but today I know. Come into my life. Unwrap my pain. Take my past and resurrect me to a new life. I receive You as my Lord and Savior. In Jesus' name, Amen.

Conclusion

There Is a Champion Inside of You

But we must hold on to the progress we have already made.

Philippians 3:16

Don't lose ground,
Don't stop training,
Don't stop growing.

As I close out this final chapter, I want to speak to you as a coach. I want to encourage you to keep moving forward, to keep training and to keep growing. A coach pushes you beyond where you think you can go. I want you to reach your full potential and to know who you are in Christ. Some people are more scared of success than of failure because it raises the bar of expectation. To stay successful, you will need to have continual growth, maturity and the desire to improve. We must decide each day to prepare for our future. Preparation starts in our prayer closet, in the quiet place where we can be with the Lord. Preparation on the inside will be seen on the outside. "Practice these things, immerse yourself in them, so that all may see your progress" (1 Timothy 4:15 ESV).

God has a great purpose for your life, and you will not reach it by sitting around doing nothing. You may be waiting on the Lord, but waiting does not mean becoming stagnant. While you are waiting, you serve others. You help people and you listen for God to unveil what is next in your life.

People may not have faith in you, but you have a heavenly Father who does. Just take that in for a moment. I do not care if you have been in prison twenty years for murder. There are people in the Bible who committed murder and became champions of the faith. Remember, you cannot live in the past. If you feed your past, you are going to starve your future. Close the book on it. You cannot change it. There is no redo. If you keep talking about the past, you are never going to dream about what is to come. You have hope because you have been forgiven. Start a new chapter in your journey with God. There is so much more He has for you ahead!

> Don't you realize that in a race everyone runs, but only one person gets the prize? So run to win! All athletes are disciplined in their training. They do it to win a prize that will fade away, but we do it for an eternal prize.
>
> 1 Corinthians 9:24–25

All of us are in the human race. Some days we may feel as if we want to quit, but we need to keep moving forward. Like a track athlete who is running a race, we are called to stay in our own lane. I am not trying to get in your lane and in your business. I am focused on staying in my lane, where I am clear to run at my pace. I am not going to look all around the track for you. That would cause me to become distracted. I am not going to stress about how far ahead of me you are. My purpose is to finish my race, not your race. I am not comparing myself to anyone else. If I am running with purpose, I am living with purpose.

And how do you run to win? You submit, like an athlete, to strict discipline. Now, I know that you may not like the thought of becoming disciplined in areas of your life. As a coach, I need to tell you that you do not accomplish great things unless you are disciplined. Big things do not happen with lazy habits. If you cannot be disciplined, how can God hand you something that needs diligent tending to grow? Are you currently capable of holding on to what He gives you and nurturing it to maturity? Should God invest in you? If you were a stock on the stock market, should God (or anyone, really) invest in you?

BIG THINGS DO NOT HAPPEN WITH LAZY HABITS.

Make a decision to start your training today. Start with accountability in the areas of your life that need improvement. Do you currently have an accountability partner? If not, get one. Find someone you trust to hold you accountable. This is a great place to start your training. Do not get sick of training or grow weary of waking up early. I hope you realize that we train to run our race for something that will last forever. There is an eternal reward in heaven.

Now let's talk about discipline. Discipline is having a schedule and sticking to it. Discipline takes training. We discipline our body by resisting the flesh. We do not let our flesh distract us or pull us out of alignment with God's plan. Life may have detours, and things may happen to try to disqualify us from God's will for our lives, but these are the perfect times to push forward in our race and make a straight line to the finish.

I often tell myself that I am a boxer who does not waste his punches. Have you ever seen a fighter in a boxing match miss their opponent? Missing punches wears you out. It takes more energy when you miss a punch. The more I train, the less I will miss. Discipline is having a schedule and sticking to it.

We need to take our walk with the Lord very seriously. Maybe you have questioned your Christianity because the person who led you to the Lord is not living for God anymore. It is very sad and hurts deeply when a Christian does foolish things and makes careless decisions. It can cause others to stumble. You need to be very careful with your Christian walk, and this takes the development of discipline.

Life Truths

Let me give you four life truths:

The Christian walk was never promised to be easy.
The person doing the right thing will eventually win.
Winners have a better attitude than losers.
A bad attitude is a choice.

As a Christian, I know that as long as I have Jesus on my side everything will be fine. Whatever I am going through, He is right there with me. There is a purpose and a reason I am walking through difficult situations.

The Christian life is not easy. You are going to have to push yourself through some quitting points and realize there is a champion inside of you. You do not become a champion when someone says you are one; you become a champion when you see it in yourself. You have got to believe in yourself.

Do not judge people in the middle of their race. God is not going to judge us in the middle of it. He is going to judge us at the end of it. In the middle of the race, we may fall. We may stumble and get hurt. We may do the wrong things or say the wrong things. But do not judge. Instead, offer help. The goal is to complete the race.

Attitude is so important. A positive attitude is a choice you must make every day. A winner is someone who says, "I have a plan." A loser is someone who says, "I have an excuse." A winner says, "Let me help." A loser says, "It is not my job."

Winners know how big God is, and losers look at how big the problem is. Excuses do not get you paid, and they do not get you a better job. Excuses surely will not get you a promotion. Every chance you get, hang around people who can sharpen you. Do not be intimidated by them. Just listen to what they have to say. Look for people who will improve your life.

Winning does not give you the attitude of a champion. The attitude is what makes you a winner. Winners act like champions. Winners set goals. They set personal goals, marriage and family goals, spiritual goals, educational goals and life goals. They continually seek to improve their lives and invest in themselves and others.

Champions know that how they think will make a difference between winning and losing. Every day we have a choice to quit or to keep enduring. Please understand that our choices will affect future generations.

- Champions understand their calling and are willing to be raised up for revival.
- Champions are driven.

- Champions are never satisfied with where they are.
- Champions are made, not born.

You and I were not born winners and losers. We are what we push ourselves to believe. Individually, you are in control of the greatness inside you. You can choose how you will view yourself. Sometimes we can be too hard on ourselves, and it is in those times that we can appreciate someone acting as a coach to us who says that they believe in us. We need fellow Christians around us who will speak that kind of life into us, to lead us to the cross and to pray with us and for us.

Likewise, we need to be prepared to be the coach for other believers. We should always be on the lookout for those around us who need to be encouraged. Linking arms and lifting each other up is vital.

Look, today you may be thinking, *I'm the one who needs to be encouraged. This season has been too hard for me! I need to be lifted up.* I want you to know that allowing Jesus to carry you is not a sign of weakness. Sometimes we have to be carried off the playing field of life and nurtured back to health so that we can get back in the race and finish it.

As your coach today, I want you to make a decision that you will cross the finish line—even with the pain you are currently experiencing—versus not finishing the race at all. Quitting is never an option. There is a champion inside of you. I am so proud of you! I know with a heart on fire that you will accomplish all God has set before you!

Let's pray this prayer together:

Lord, I let go of all the areas of my life that are holding me back. I will not allow pain and hurt to keep me from my purpose. I surrender all of the hurting places in my heart to You and know that You are my Healer. I know that You have predestined me for greatness. This is my time, this is my moment. I rebuke all failure and disappointment in my life. I believe I am a champion. I will no longer believe the lies of the devil. I believe that You have given me a heart on fire for You and for Your people. I know You love me, and You understand everything that I have gone through. I am going to finish this race You have set before me. I am going to finish strong. I openly receive all of the promises You have set before me. I ask You, Lord, for more passion, for miracles, signs and wonders to take place all around me. I ask You to help me find my purpose. Help me to dream big dreams, and motivate me to do all You have called me to do. Use me to reach my loved ones and my city for Christ. I believe I will bring revival with me everywhere I go. I believe I was chosen to change the world. In Jesus' name, Amen!

Notes

Chapter 2 Fed Up, Filled Up and Fired Up

1. This is a paraphrased story taken primarily from 1 Corinthians 15:6 and Acts 1:15.

Chapter 6 How to Have a Rain Revival

1. Matt Erikson, "Old Camel Knees: A Brief Reflection on the Remarkable Prayer Life of James the Just," *MWErickson.com*, August 29, 2019, https://mwerickson.com/2019/08/29/old-camel-knees-a-brief-reflection -on-the-remarkable-prayer-life-of-james-the-just/.

Chapter 8 How to Have a Wind Revival

1. Hope Bolinger, "Why Does Ezekiel Prophecy to a Valley of Dry Bones?" *Crosswalk.com*, March 4, 2021, https://www.crosswalk.com /faith/bible-study/why-does-ezekiel-prophecy-to-dry-bones.html.

Chapter 9 How to Have a Fire Revival

1. Sami K. Martin, "Student Ordered to Remove Cross Necklace by University: 'We Need to Fight Back,'" *ChristianPost.com*, July 5, 2013, https://www.christianpost.com/news/student-ordered-to-remove-cross -necklace-by-university-we-need-to-fight-back-99448.

2. Steve Novak, *LehighValleyLive.com*, May 16, 2017, https://www .lehighvalleylive.com/warren-county/2017/05/teacher_who_gave_student _a_bib.html.

3. Michael Foust, "Christian Song 'Awesome God' OK in After-School Talent Show, Judge Rules," *BaptistPress.com*, December 12, 2006, https://

www.baptistpress.com/resource-library/news/christian-song-awesome
-god-ok-in-after-school-talent-show-judge-rules/.

4. Gina Meeks, "University Apologizes for Forcing Students to Stomp
on Jesus' Name, *CharismaNews.com*, March 26, 2013, https://www
.charismanews.com/us/38833-university-apologizes-for-forcing-students
-to-stomp-on-jesus-name.

5. Joshua Rhett Miller, "Georgia Mayor Hopes to End Flap Over
Prayer Before Meals at Senior Center," *FoxNews.com*, December 1,
2015, https://www.foxnews.com/us/georgia-mayor-hopes-to-end-flap
-over-prayer-before-meals-at-senior-center.

6. Leonardo Blair, "High School Forces Christian Valedictorian to
Remove References to Jesus, Faith From Speech," *ChristianPost.com*,
May 23, 2018, https://www.christianpost.com/news/high-school-forces
-christian-valedictorian-to-remove-references-to-jesus-faith-from-speech
.html.

7. Todd Starnes, "Military Blocks Access to Southern Baptist Convention Website," *ChristianPost.com*, April 25, 2013, https://www.christian
post.com/news/military-blocks-access-to-southern-baptist-convention
-website.html.

8. Katherine Weber, "10-Year-Old's 'God is my Idol' Assignment Now
Accepted By Tenn. School; Given 100 Percent After Rejection Backlash,"
ChristianPost.com, October 20, 2013, https://www.christianpost.com/news
/10-year-olds-god-is-my-idol-assignment-now-accepted-by-tenn-school
-given-100-percent-after-rejection-backlash.html.

9. "Constitution of the State of California," *CPP.edu*, 1879, https://
www.cpp.edu/~jlkorey/calcon1879.pdf.

Chapter 11 The Part You Play in Revival

1. Alexandra Deabler, "Woman Denied Outback Steakhouse Attacks
Parents, Threatens to 'Kill' Them," *FoxNews.com*, January 6, 2019,
https://www.foxnews.com/food-drink/woman-denied-outback-steak
house-attacks-parents-threatens-to-kill-them.

2. Associated Press, "Boy, 12, Found Guilty in Shooting Death of Mom
After Fight Over Chores," *FoxNews.com*, January 14, 2015, https://www
.foxnews.com/story/boy-12-found-guilty-in-shooting-death-of-mom
-after-fight-over-chores.

3. "14-Year-Old Detroit Boy Shoots Mom While She Sleeps: Reports,"
HuffPost.com, February 28, 2012, https://www.huffpost.com/entry/14
-year-old-son-shoots-mom-detroit-tamiko-robinson_n_1304705.

4. CBS News Staff, "Murder in the First Grade," *CBSnews.com*, March
7, 2000, https://www.cbsnews.com/news/murder-in-the-first-grade/.

5. Christina Caron, "Girl Allegedly Shoots Dad for Taking Cell Phone, Police Say," *ABCNews.Go.com*, May 26, 2011, https://abcnews.go.com/US /girl-shoots-dad-taking-cell-phone-police/story?id=13695008.

6. Jenni Fink, "11-Year-Old Allegedly Shot Dad in Back, Said There Would Be 'Part Two'" If He Didn't Get PlayStation, Xbox," *Newsweek .com*, March 18, 2019, https://www.newsweek.com/11-year-old-alleg edly-shot-dad-back-said-there-would-be-part-two-if-he-didnt-1356721.

7. Natalie Ktena, "These Teens Secretly Trolled Themselves Online," *BBC.Co.UK*, May 18, 2018, https://www.bbc.co.uk/bbcthree/article /05e9991d-4713-4ad4-b9af-eecd47d7dfd7.

8. Weekend Edition Sunday, "The Risk of Teen Depression and Suicide Is Linked to Smartphone Use, Study Says," NPR.org, December 17, 2017, https://www.npr.org/2017/12/17/571443683/the-call-in-teens -and-depression.

Glen Berteau is an evangelist, teacher and author. He and his wife, Deborah, are also the founding pastors of The House Churches. The House Network of Churches comprises of more than fifty churches in the United States and around the world. They have started over 25 Bible schools in Cambodia.

They were the senior pastors of The House Modesto, in Modesto, California, for over thirty years. Their ministry in Central California has been life-changing for the city and the people of that community. Between all outreaches at The House Modesto, over 160,000 people have been won to the Lord.

Glen was a high school all-American running back and accepted a scholarship to Louisiana Tech University. As a four-year starter, he was All Conference, won two national championships and was Most Outstanding Back for three out of four years.

During his freshman year in college, someone told Glen he needed to be saved to go to heaven. Glen responded, "Saved from what?" On April 30, 1973, his junior year, he knelt on the floor of his dormitory room floor and accepted Jesus Christ.

A few years later, he became a youth pastor and established one of the largest youth ministries in the nation. During that season, he wrote the youth manual, *Strategies for Advancing Youth Ministries*. He also wrote the books *Christianity Lite* and *Christianity To Go* with Charisma House.

As a gifted speaker and teacher, Glen ministers at conferences, events, churches and conventions all over the world.

Glen holds three master's degrees in practical theology (Southeastern University), pastoral ministry (The King's University) and ministerial leadership (Trinity Theological Seminary).

On November 25, 2019, in the parking lot of The House Modesto, Glen had a cardiac arrest and died. Following the lack of oxygen and trauma to his body from the repeated electric shocks that revived him, his chance of survival was extremely slim. He had just completed his book with Chosen Books, *Why Am I Not Healed? (When God Promised)*. He is a walking, talking miracle that science cannot explain. His resurrection story was featured on *The 700 Club* and is described as miraculous survival.

Glen and his wife, Deborah, have three children and eight grandchildren. They live in Colleyville, Texas. Learn more about Glen and his work at glenberteau.com.

More from Glen Berteau

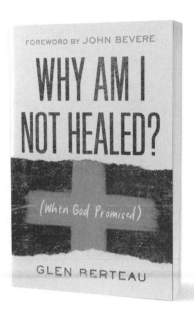

Is it God's *will* to heal? And is it God's will to heal *you*? Pastor Glen Berteau approaches these questions with compassion and hope. Countering seventeen hindrances to prayer for healing, he breaks through possible misunderstanding regarding God's good intentions for His children. Your faith has the power to move mountains—why settle for less?

Why Am I Not Healed?